Marx and Human Nature

Marx and Human Nature

Refutation of a Legend

NORMAN GERAS

VERSO

London · New York

First published by Verso 1983
© Norman Geras 1983
All rights reserved
Second impression 1994

Verso
UK: 6 Meard Street, London W1V 3HR
USA: 29 West 35th Street, New York, NY 10001–2291

Verso is the imprint of New Left Books

ISBN 978-0-86091-066-4

British Library Cataloguing in Publication Data
A catalogue record for this book is available from the British Library

Library of Congress Cataloging-in-Publication Data
A catalogue record for this book is available from the Library of Congress

Typeset in Bembo by Preface Ltd, Salisbury, Wiltshire
Printed in Great Britain by Biddles Ltd

Contents

Contents

TO ADÈLE

. . .as is well known, a spark
dazzles rather than
illuminates: nothing is
more difficult to locate in the
darkness of the night than
the point of light which
breaks it.

–Louis Althusser

Foreword

This short essay attempts to dispose once and for all of a rather obstinate old legend about the thought of Karl Marx. So far at least as these things do depend upon the marshalling of sound evidence and argument, that aim is not excessively ambitious. For the legend is certainly false. I hope to have provided here both evidence and argument enough to demonstrate its falsehood. In any case, it is the hope of a conclusive refutation that accounts for features of the essay of which it would be as well to inform the reader in advance. Some brief remarks on how it was originally conceived will serve this purpose.

You will not go very far in discussion either within or about Marxism before encountering the view that one of the things bequeathed to this intellectual tradition by its founder was a denial of the idea of a universal human nature. That view, which had already had a good life when Althusser's 'theoretical anti-humanism' imparted to it a new confidence and vigour, has long struck me as being pretty remarkable, and it was my attendance at a certain seminar one evening in early 1979 that led me to want to confront it. The seminar, in fact, was not about Marx or about Marxism. It was on the subject of human needs. I no longer recall the details of the discussion, only that the theoretical and practical viability of a concept of common human needs was received with general scepticism, and this was sustained in part – or so it appeared to me – by impulses of a relativist and idealist kind. Since much of both philosophy and social science is thick with relativist and idealist themes, there is perhaps no great cause for puzzlement here. Nevertheless, the occasion did crystallize in my mind the thought of how surprising it was that Marxists also, would-be materialists amongst them, should often sponsor more or less similar themes in support of a similar scepticism; how very extraordinary indeed, in view of what I had read in Marx, in view equally of some obvious facts about the world, that the claim that he rejected the idea of human nature should be so widely made and believed.

I decided to look and see just what from Marx's work is generally given as confirmation of the claim. The answer is: not very much – actually only a single passage that can be said to amount to anything, though Marx himself did not think fit to publish the text containing it; and, apart from that, a few other odds and ends which, considered for the role of evidence in this matter, amount to nothing at all. The one item of any plausibility is some lines from the *Theses on Feuerbach* and it is with a close and extended analysis of those lines that I have chosen therefore to begin the present study. Some may perhaps find this analysis rather too extended and wonder why, when so much in Marx's writings can be brought against the claim in question, I was not content simply to appeal to that and to see off the passage from the *Theses* with more dispatch. I would ask only that they postpone judgment of the opening analysis until they have digested what follows it. I hope the sequel will persuade them of its point.

Here it will suffice to say this much. There are already

plenty of commentaries on Marx which draw attention to this contrary evidence. Nothing was to be gained by just repeating them. However, by focusing initially on the best of the textual support for the disputed claim, we first square up to the latter on its own chosen terrain, so to speak, meet it at what may be supposed to be its strong point. From doing this, as it happens, there is something to be gained. It may be a few lines only that become thereby an object of detailed attention, but they have been made to bear a heavy weight in the exegesis of Marx. Relying on their support, the legend that he dispensed with the concept of an intrinsic human nature manages to survive in the face of textual evidence that he did not: either this is simply ignored or else, if its existence is conceded, it is treated as the basis merely of one 'reading' of Marx to which however another, alternative 'reading' can be opposed, or else it is said not to represent the real, or the most profound, tendency of his mature thought; and so on. Yet, examination of the relevant lines from the *Theses on Feuerbach* reveals that their sense is not, in fact, transparent. They can be understood in a number of ways. And when the various possible meanings of this passage are placed within the only possible context for its proper assessment, the interpretation of Marx that has been so reliant on it is shown not to be a viable one at all. It is left without even the slenderest title to philological respectability.

A second feature of my approach here of which notice should be given is that I take this interpretation at its word. The argument that Marx rejected all concepts of a universal human nature is construed in its literal sense. For, its advocates do themselves emphasize that what he opposed was not just this or that view about human nature but the very idea of one, and it is only this emphasis, moreover, that justifies presentation of the argument as though it were a theoretically bold and momentous one and told us something distinctive about him. Such it would scarcely either be or do if the proposition was merely that Marx dismissed some conceptions of human nature. Of whom is that not true? I am aware, all the same, that construing this particular argument in a straightforward way lends an air of strangeness, a certain unreality, to parts of the discussion, and this might prompt the suggestion that it would be intellectually more charitable therefore, and the claim more credible, if one took a narrower view than I do here of what counts as a concept of human nature. Now, of course, should we choose to include under this heading just those conceptions of an enduring and common human make-up with which Marx did in fact disagree, but not any that he, for his part, entertained, then the claim will appear very credible indeed. However, I can think of no genuinely compelling reason for doing this. Intellectually charitable it certainly is, but it gives us a definition that is eccentric and, worse, tendentious: selected with the claim in mind; purposely designed for the rescue of a bad, albeit widely used, argument. The view taken in this essay of what is to count as a concept of human nature is, on the contrary, a quite standard one. It is one that is found, as we shall see, in Marx's own usage. Most importantly, it is the one embodied in what the claim's advocates actually say, for all that this renders their claim unreasonable. It is better to be true to what they say than to be charitable to it. And it is more than time. This is a case like that of *The Emperor's New Clothes*. The argument is given out as though it were a sober and serious intellectual position. So, too, is it frequently received. But once you take it seriously, once you examine it for what it is, it is seen then to be, precisely, unreasonable.

Marx – like everyone else – did reject certain ideas of

human nature; but he also regarded some as being true. It is important to discriminate the sort that he rejected from the sort that he did not. More important still is it to try to discriminate such of these ideas as are indeed true from such of them as are false. Neither purpose is served by talk of the dismissal of all conceptions of a human nature, and I hope the essay here may contribute something to replacing it by more limited but, at the same time, more accurate statements of what, in this matter, Marx actually opposed.

The foregoing explanations will make plain enough that this study is not very kind to the interpretation of Marx that is its object. For this I make no apology; I do not think the criticism it offers unfair. From what has been said, however, it should not be inferred that I can see no valid preoccupation whatever amongst the factors that have led many Marxists at least to persuade themselves of this interpretation. In the final section of the essay, when consideration of the textual materials has been concluded, I examine the reasons that dispose people to want to deny the existence of a human nature. Although my main purpose is to show that they are not good ones, I do say, wherever I think there are grounds for doing so, what legitimate concern any particular argument may exaggerate or in some other way reflect. To give one example, whilst I criticize the oft-expressed belief that the concept of human nature is simply reactionary, I acknowledge nonetheless that there are reactionary variants of it, as well as how frequently these are met with.

This may well be the principal obstacle to a readier acceptance of the concept amongst those committed to fundamental and progressive change: conservative and reactionary assumptions about what is inherent in humanity's make-up are pervasive. That they are owes a lot, probably, to the historical influence of the Christian doctrine of original sin, but there are other doctrinal sources aplenty, secular as well as religious, new beside old, for assumptions of innate human wickedness and belief, correspondingly, in the permanence of social malignancy of one kind or another. Such ideas close off the avenues of thought against the prospect of liberation from manifold social oppressions. Their pervasiveness, relative to progressive conceptions of human nature, must perhaps always be the norm while class society survives. A long past and continuing present of exploitation and its associated evils will tend to yield pessimistic generalizations about the character traits and typical behaviour of human beings. Anyone who has tried to present socialism as a serious practical proposition before virtually any audience not already convinced of it, will almost certainly have had to contend with pessimistic argument from 'human nature'.

And yet to attempt to respond to that kind of argument, and to the weight of conservative culture supporting it, by denying that there is a human nature, is to meet a powerful ideological opponent with a weapon that is useless. Not only this or that ideology, but also widely accessible facts and truths – some derived from common experience, others the product of scientific research – will tell one's interlocutors that this is foolishness. A proper regard for what are the real basic needs and capacities inherent in our human nature is the only adequate response.

Many people have helped me during the writing of this essay. For advice, comment and discussion, my thanks are due, and are herewith tendered, to Perry Anderson, David Beetham, Robin Blackburn, Gerry Cohen, Alistair Edwards, Michael Evans, Adèle Geras, Ian Gough, Fred Halliday, Harry Lesser, Caroline McCulloch, David McLellan, Tony Manstead, Peter Morriss, Raymond

Plant, David-Hillel Ruben, Ian Steedman, Hillel Steiner and Ursula Vogel. None of them is responsible for any of the work's deficiencies.

I want also to thank Sophie Geras and Jenny Geras for being both tolerant and remarkably patient on a number of occasions when my priorities did not coincide with theirs.

Manchester, December 1982.

Introduction

Whatever might separate Marx's intellectual development after 1845 from the themes of his early writings, it is not that he came to reject the idea of a human nature.

In this essay I devote close scrutiny to the sixth of Marx's *Theses on Feuerbach,* widely cited as evidence that he did so. My purpose is to discredit its status as evidence. In pursuit of this objective I show that Marx's later writings unambiguously do embody the idea in question, which fulfils both explanatory and normative functions.

This should not really need to be shown. To anyone who has read his later writings with a minimum of care, the claim that Marx's well-known emphases on historical specificity and historical change did not detach him from every general conception of human nature may seem too obvious to be worth the proof. A number of careful, albeit differing, treatments of his theory of history have already made the point clearly enough.[1] Against this, however, must be set the widespread influence of Althusser and his school in disseminating a belief to the contrary. Such a belief is especially prevalent amongst Marxists. It is indeed an old fixation, which the Althusserian influence in this matter has fed upon, that there is no place within historical materialism for the concept of a human nature. Because this fixation still exists and is misguided, it is still necessary to challenge it.

I begin (I) by specifying how the term 'human nature' is used here. The essay then proceeds from (II) analysis of the sixth thesis itself to (III) a consideration of its place within Marx's work as a whole. Finally (IV) some other items of putative evidence for the view of Marx to be contested here and some arguments commonly directed against the idea of a human nature are reviewed in turn and criticized as unsound.

I
Definitions

Two ways in which it is customary to speak about 'human nature' may be distinguished. In the first, one purports to refer by the term to a constant entity, to qualities of human beings that are all but universal, amongst nature's regularities so to say, and not part of the variety of history. This is typically what is involved in claims that human nature rules out the possibility of socialism, lasting human harmony, direct democracy and what have you. In a second usage, however, the same term can denote a variable entity as when it is said that human nature is different in different times or places or according to the influence of different circumstances. The idea here is of a historically changing, socio-culturally specific entity.

I am not sure if these usages must actually entail two distinct meanings of the term 'human nature'. We could perhaps just understand it as signifying broadly 'the character of human beings', and recognize that one can assert of this character that it is a constant one, or that it is a changing one, or indeed that it is a complex of variant and invariant features, and so on. Something like this broad sense is what a closely related locution, 'the nature of man', is often used to convey.

But perhaps because repeated assertions of invariance

have helped to associate the idea with it, the term 'human nature' can, I think, also carry an implication of invariance as part of its very meaning. One can deny, for example, that belief in God, or the desire to accumulate property and power, or apathy towards public affairs, is actually a feature of human nature, knowing that each of these is a significant element in the character of human beings in a wide variety of circumstances; the claim is that they are not permanent or general human characteristics. That is to construe 'human nature' more narrowly. Again, the not uncommon assertion amongst Marxists, 'There is no (such thing as) human nature', surely relies on this narrower meaning. It challenges the existence of a human character that is constant.

In any case, for clarity of argument I observe a terminological artifice and discriminate systematically between the expressions 'human nature' and 'the nature of man'. Throughout this essay, save once above for illustrative purposes, I use 'human nature' only when I intend to denote a constant entity, namely, the set of all (relatively)[2] permanent and general human characteristics. Otherwise I speak of 'the nature of man', employing this, in the broader sense I have identified, to mean the all-round character of human beings in some given context. Whilst the first usage makes of *human nature* something unchanging by definition – though there can be argument about whether there is such a thing – the second leaves open the degree of mutability in *the nature of man*. This may be more or less variable. It will not exclude what anthropological constants there are, if there are any.

Where it may not be clear, and I wish to leave undetermined, which of these expressions is the appropriate one – as transpires in the immediate sequel at the beginning of my treatment of the sixth thesis – there I talk of 'man's "nature" ', or resort to some other phrase wherein the key word is bounded thus by scare-quotes as a mark of its indeterminacy. Unless otherwise indicated, 'man', 'men', etc. are used in the generic sense to include both sexes. I have adopted this usage for ease and consistency of exposition only, in circumstances where reference has constantly to be made to textual excerpts translated in accordance with the same usage.

II
The Sixth Thesis

Here is the sixth of Marx's *Theses on Feuerbach:*

> 'Feuerbach resolves the essence of religion into the essence of *man*. But the essence of man is no abstraction inherent in each single individual. In its reality it is the ensemble of the social relations.
>
> 'Feuerbach, who does not enter upon a criticism of this real essence, is hence obliged:
>
> '1. To abstract from the historical process and to define the religious sentiment by itself, and to presuppose an abstract – *isolated* – human individual.
>
> '2. Essence, therefore, can be regarded only as "species", as an inner, mute, general character which unites the many individuals *in a natural way.*'

The main burden of Marx's criticism is quite straightforward. Feuerbach's conception of religion is characterized as being ahistorical and asocial: he locates the source of religion within the human individual as such, abstracted from any social formation. I leave aside whether or not the criticism is an accurate one. But the accents in which it is registered should be familiar to Marx's readers: on history relative to nature; on social relations relative to the individual; on the social reality 'out there' as it were, relative to the individual's intrinsic characteristics. In the next of the *Theses,* the seventh, Marx continues in essentially the same vein: 'Feuerbach, consequently, does not see that the "religious sentiment" is itself a social product, and that the abstract individual which he analyses belongs to a particular form of society.'[3]

If we do not go beyond the letter of these few lines, however, there are also ambiguities in them, particularly in those propositions which either state or imply something about man's 'essence'.

The German expression Marx employs is 'das menschliche Wesen'. Translators of the sixth thesis have usually rendered it as 'the essence of man' or 'the human essence'. In other places in his work it is sometimes translated as 'human nature'.[4] It is common for interpreters to assume that the sixth thesis is concerned with human nature, be it directly, because that is just what 'Wesen' refers to there, or indirectly, having a bearing upon it by being about the nature of man. I shall take it that this assumption is correct or at least harmless: that Marx was speaking about human nature, either directly or by discussing the nature of man; or else had in mind something as close to one of these two things as will make no difference. If the assumption is not correct and Marx's interest on this occasion was remote from both of them, this cannot damage the position I defend. On the contrary, it is so much the worse for those who claim Marx broke with the idea of a human nature, since their main candidate for a serious piece of evidence is then disqualified. I avoid proliferation and confusion of terms, therefore, as also any special metaphysical connotations which the word 'essence' might suggest in this context, by dispensing with it in favour of the two expressions I have defined.

Holding it for the moment open which of them is the

appropriate one, let us consider in turn the critical and the negative characterizations of man's 'nature' embodied, respectively, in the last and the second sentences of the thesis, before attempting to construe the positive identification of it which the third sentence contains.

Notice, then, that in the final sentence Marx takes Feuerbach to task for conceiving man's 'nature' *only* as species, as an inner generality uniting individuals in a natural way. Marx does not say that it is *not* these things. The sentence permits the interpretation that, for Marx, Feuerbach is mistaken not because he views man in terms of 'inner', 'general', 'species' (or 'natural') characteristics but because he views him exclusively in those terms. He is wrong for a one-sidedness of perspective rather than wrong *tout court*. On that interpretation, Marx would here be echoing the thought he communicated to Arnold Ruge two years earlier. Feuerbach, Marx wrote, 'refers too much to nature and too little to politics.'[5]

Still, the construction of the sentence under discussion cannot rule out that Marx's reproach might be the sterner one: that Feuerbach is wholly mistaken to conceive man's 'nature' in such terms. Some will deem this improbable, an opinion I comment upon in due course, but let us stay with the bare construction. To remark, critically, that in some deficient conception, '*A* can be (or is) regarded only as *B*', is to the point when *A* is not *B* as well as when *A* is *B* but not only *B*. It can be a way of denying *A*'s *B*–hood and not merely of qualifying it. Consider two examples. If I say, in argument against a well-known view of capitalism, 'The relation of capitalist and worker is regarded only as a contractual one between legally equal persons', I need not in this case intend to deny that the relationship is as described; I can be alluding to important additional features of it, in particular that it is a relation of exploitation.

On the other hand, should I say, 'On such-and-such assumptions (wild ones), Marx can be regarded only as a fool', my point would be that Marx was not a fool, rather than that he was other things as well as a fool. Is it possible to resolve whether Marx meant on this occasion to reject, or whether he meant only to qualify, a conception of man in terms of inner, general, species characteristics?

Let us examine the second sentence of the thesis. There is a sort of internal link between it and the final sentence. If man's 'nature' dwelt within each individual, it would have that inner and universal character which the final sentence *perhaps* denies it to have. The second sentence on the face of it does contain such a denial: man's 'nature', according to Marx, 'is no abstraction inherent in each single individual'. This seems quite categorical and so, keeping still to the letter, it may be. But even keeping to the letter, it need not. Despite the explicit negative in this sentence, what Marx says does not have to entail a belief that man's 'nature' is flatly *not* inherent in the single individual. Formulations of the kind, '*A* is no *B*; it is *C*', are used, it is true, for conveying just this type of categorical denial. 'The wage relation is no injustice; it is a free and mutually beneficial exchange between equals'; and 'Marx was no fool; he was a profound and original thinker' – these may serve to exemplify that usage. They exploit the starkness of contrast between two characterizations of a subject as a way of rebutting one of them. Concede it as a possibility, then, that Marx's thought, in counterposing to the individual 'the ensemble of the social relations', might have been: man's 'nature' is not, at all or in any aspect, an 'abstraction inherent in each single individual'. That, however, is not the only possibility.

For, '*A* is no *B*' can also have the force '*A* is no *mere B*'. It just depends on what it is that follows. If it is a description of *A* not manifestly opposed to the one that has gone before, the sense can be, roughly, that *A* is not only *B* because *A* is *more* than *B* in a loose sense of the word 'more'; because, comprehended roundly, *A* is *C*. Compare these two statements: 'Religion is no opiate; it is a genuine enrichment of the human spirit'; and 'Religion is no inward, private, spiritual affair; it is an ensemble of institutions and practices pervading the public order'. An advocate of the first claim, if we impute to her a standard attitude towards opiates, would be gainsaying that way of describing religion. An advocate of the second claim is unlikely, at any rate not bound, to be gainsaying that religion is inward and private and spiritual in common senses of these words. She could and probably would just be asserting that, as a pervasive institutional and practical reality, religion is more than what they tend to convey, and wanting to register the importance, perhaps priority, of its external and public features. Here is another example. I could say, 'Language is no individual possession; it is a social and collective phenomenon', without supposing, absurdly, that it is not individuals who know and speak, to that extent 'possess', a language. The point in these cases is not to deny, it is to qualify a given description, by bringing to the fore some other, putatively crucial, dimension of the subject of the description.

Now, social relations are obviously something different from the single individual and what is inherent in him. On a certain conceptual terrain, the difference, hence the contrast at the heart of the sixth thesis, might be at least as sharp as those, in the above examples, between a mutually beneficial exchange and an injustice, a profound thinker and a fool, an enrichment of the human spirit and an opiate. On the other hand, the human individual does figure prominently amongst the entities which social relations relate and could be reckoned a part, or feature, of them. One should therefore allow that, in identifying man's 'nature' with the social relations at large, Marx's intention might have been not that it is entirely other, but that it is 'more', than something inherent in each single individual. Another side of the counterpoint in these lines tends to support this possibility. For, they refer us not only from what is inherent in the individual to the social relations, but also from the abstraction of the first to the ensemble, the totality, of the second. The sense of 'abstraction' that is suggested by this is the one made explicit by Marx a few lines further on: of a thing *isolated;* separated, as a part from the whole of which it is a part, and by virtue of that, one-sided.

Read in this light, the second sentence of the thesis would be comparable to my examples concerning the public, or societal, aspect of religion and of language. The sense would be: man's 'nature' is not *just* the abstract thing (i.e., the abstracted, one-sidedly isolated entity) inherent within each single individual; and not that it is not at all something inherent. The sentence is consistent with believing man's 'nature' to be, in *some* aspects, intrinsic to each individual and thus universal. Marx could have been wanting to temper this belief by drawing attention to other aspects of man's 'nature'. He does not, by this utterance, have to have been contradicting it.[6]

Yet I have already conceded also that he might have been. By examining the second sentence of the thesis, we have not therefore resolved the ambiguity we identified in its final sentence. We still have that: either Marx was here rejecting altogether a conception of man's 'nature' in terms of inherent and general human characteristics; or else he was only qualifying it. Let us style these possibilities respectively the stern and the mild interpretation of the two sentences.

One might perhaps be tempted to settle in favour of the mild interpretation by this line of thought, alluded to earlier and bound to have occurred to some readers. That there are general human characteristics inherent in each individual, irrespective of the ensemble of social relations (or the 'particular form of society'), is not only true but obviously so. The denial of this is not just, equally obviously, false. It is absurd, involving, as I shall argue later, a logical incoherence. As Marx was no fool, he surely could not have intended such a denial in the sixth thesis. But it would be wrong, however tempting in this case, to assume that, simply because something is false or incoherent, Marx could not have intended it. That Marx must have believed what is true is no more plausible as a supposition than that what Marx believed must be true. Both suppositions have already obfuscated enough issues. Serious people have understood him as intending here precisely the aforesaid denial, and some of them have endorsed his intention so understood. So far as we have been able to go up to now, we must allow that Marx too, even though no fool, might have erred in this matter.

Since our consideration of what is said negatively about man's 'nature' has left things unresolved, let us hope for better results from turning to the central affirmative proposition contained in the third sentence. We render it, initially, thus: 'In its reality man's "nature" is the ensemble of social relations'. The peculiarity of this proposition has often been remarked upon. Marx asserts an identity where none seems possible: between a totality of relations on the one hand, and the make-up of entities that are related by and within it on the other. However one conceptualizes an ensemble of social relations with respect to the individual human beings and to the non-human factors (means of production, property holdings, etc.) that it brings into relation; if one takes it as including them; *a fortiori* if, on the grounds that it is a structure and that a structure may be defined as excluding the terms of the relations which constitute it,[7] one does not; in either case, the 'nature' of the human beings cannot just *be* the ensemble of social relations. Whether by their 'nature' is meant only the characteristics of their human nature or, rather, all those that compose their overall character, there is no obvious sense in which this set of characteristics can be the same thing as an ensemble of social relations. Like much else in the *Theses on Feuerbach* Marx's statement is elliptical and his meaning far from transparent.

In what follows I shall propose broadly three ways of understanding it: I elicit them by attention to and argument from the text, and then enlarge somewhat upon each; I go on to impugn the exegetical plausibility of the only one of these three meanings that supports the stern interpretation of the other two sentences. First I want to forestall a likely objection.

This is that it must be vain to hope to settle the issue before us by intensive scrutiny of one small group, especially this small group, of words. In general, a sentence can yield only so much of a person's thought and no more. In particular, the peculiarity of Marx's third sentence suggests it will be recalcitrant to settling anything definitively, which would not be surprising in view of the condensed and aphoristic character of the *Theses on Feuerbach,* for which character they are, indeed, renowned. Add to this that the *Theses* were not published in Marx's lifetime nor intended by him for publication,[8] that they cannot therefore be authoritative in deciding a large question regarding his thought, and one may wonder whether any part of them can be worth the kind of close attention being given here. Are not the difficulties with such a procedure already evident in the foregoing discussion? In isolation from the wider context of Marx's ideas, analysis of a single sentence is as likely to generate as it is to resolve ambiguity.

The substance of the objection is sound, nor will I attempt to rest everything on scrutiny of Marx's third sentence on its own. All the same, as was indicated at the very outset, the sixth thesis has been widely construed in the sense I mean to impugn and, authoritative or not by rights, thus construed it has been, in fact, chief support of the view that, in laying down his mature theory of history, Marx discarded the concept of human nature. It is therefore as well, before considering other textual evidence, to try to unravel just what the thesis could be saying. As it happens, the sense so often ascribed to it is put thereby in some doubt. Setting the results of this exercise beside the rest of the evidence then shows that common ascription to be mistaken.

We have assumed Marx to be speaking here either about (i) *human nature,* defined as constant, or about (ii) *the nature of man* in our broader, more inclusive sense; though hitherto we have left it open which. We must now consider each alternative. We must also consider what type of relationship the third sentence is meant to establish between one or other of them and the ensemble of social relations. If it cannot be a strict identity, what can Marx have intended? An obvious consequence of the relationship he asserts is the claim: without reference to the ensemble of social relations one cannot *understand* man's 'nature'. What follows in the sixth and seventh theses permits this inference, for it is argued there that Feuerbach neglects the ensemble of social relations and for that reason commits the errors he does in his treatment of man.

However, the claim so inferred lacks precision. It requires attention to the social relations, certainly. But it could mean simply that this is where one has to look in order to grasp what the 'nature' of human beings is. Or it could embody the stronger, because explanatory, hypothesis that such attention is necessary in order to understand *why* their 'nature' is as it is. This stronger claim presupposes that it is what it is because the social relations somehow make it so, or shape it. It presupposes a type of dependence. It may be, therefore, that the third sentence is meant to affirm such a relationship between the two things, and in that case I say, provisionally, that the one 'depends upon' the other, meaning by this that the first is as it is in some degree because of the character of the second. One phrase in the seventh thesis, that 'the "religious sentiment" is itself a social product', seems to point in this direction. The other claim does not purport to explain, but only to situate, man's 'nature'. It just presupposes that the social relations as a whole form the site where that 'nature' is, roughly speaking, to be seen or found. We need not yet concern ourselves with what reasons there might be for saying this. Shortly I shall distinguish two general cases. For the moment, let us simply call the relationship thus postulated one of 'disclosure'. Much of what follows the third sentence suggests, and nothing excludes, that this rough connection is what it affirms. We allow then that Marx might have been asserting either relationship: that man's 'nature' (a) *depends upon,* or (b) *is disclosed by,* the ensemble of social relations.

Putting these with our two definitions of the subject of the sentence, we obtain:

'In its reality (i) human nature *or* (ii) the nature of man
(a) depends upon *or* (b) is disclosed by
the ensemble of social relations';

in other words four possibilities which, giving the lexical sequence priority over the numerical, I designate (a) (i), (a) (ii), (b) (i) and (b) (ii), and take now in that order.

(a) (i) *In its reality human nature depends upon the ensemble of social relations*. This possibility can be discounted. Whatever degree of dependence is meant, it would be capricious to attribute the proposition to Marx. Human nature, according to our usage, is invariant, whilst Marx's whole emphasis in the sixth and seventh theses is on the historicity and specificity, hence variability, of the ensemble of social relations. Were he speaking about human nature, he could hardly assert it to be as it is because of these changing relations. It can doubtless happen that one thing remains constant because another varies, but this contingency is in the present context uninteresting. For, if there is a human nature, a constant element in the character of human beings, it is surely not due to the social mutations between one historical epoch or mode of production and another. In principle, of course, such a constant element might be due to some invariant *aspect*, or aspects, of social relations that are otherwise variable; I discuss this below as a logical possibility consistent with another reading of the third sentence. But it seems unlikely the sentence actually asserts it in view of the stress placed upon the social relations in their totality. (a) (i) does not give Marx's meaning, so we may eliminate it.

(a) (ii) *In its reality the nature of man depends upon the ensemble of social relations*. This proposition by contrast is both intelligible and compatible with the drift of the remaining text. There seems no reason for ruling it out as a possible interpretation. The third sentence might be saying that the all-round character of human beings in any setting is what it is because of the nature of the prevailing social relations. The question then is whether that entails the denial of a human nature, and the answer will turn on the degree of dependence involved. It will be affirmative on only one of two relevant assumptions about this. Note here that we are concerned with the degree of dependence, not its precise character. As important to more comprehensive definition of historical materialism as this latter kind of issue is – and it is lucidly and exactly addressed by Gerry Cohen in the now commanding philosophical work in this area, *Karl Marx's Theory of History: A Defence* – it is not decisive for our more limited purpose. Provided the nature of man depends in *some* way consistent with our definition of dependence on the character of the social relations, all that matters is the extent to which it does so. I take it that the dependence Marx means to assert, if that is what he does mean to assert, is at least considerable. Under that description there are only two pertinently different cases: namely, that the nature of man depends strongly but not completely, and that it depends completely, on the ensemble of social relations.

In the first case, the existence of a human nature is not excluded for the obvious reason that, while the nature of man may vary substantially with, and because of, changes in the ensemble of social relations, it may also depend upon more constant factors, and some of these may constitute precisely a human nature. Now it is common enough to hold or claim that one thing depends upon another, that the second explains the first, without supposing the dependence to be total or the explanation exhaustive; knowing in other words that other explanatory factors are involved. Any of several considerations might nevertheless motivate singling out, as explanatory, just the one at the expense of all others. Three such considerations are these: a concern to highlight what is thought to be very important; a concern to highlight what risks being neglected; the presumption that some things can be taken for granted. The first two considerations seem especially to the point here. Marx is bent on criticizing and correcting a conception seen by him as entirely naturalistic, and he does so by emphatic sociological reference. The third one may seem like a piece of special pleading and as such somewhat feeble. In fact, however, it is perfectly commonplace when proffering explanation, particularly in brief compass, to take a whole background for granted and isolate only the factor(s) deemed crucial in the given discursive context as the explanation for the thing to be explained, that on which this thing may be said to depend.

Of course, were I to contend at this stage that that is just what Marx is doing in the third sentence, accentuating for contextually obvious reasons the sociological dimensions of the nature of man, whilst at the same time taking for granted other factors on which the latter depends, taking for granted, for example, certain permanent features of man's biological constitution, I should be begging the very question at issue. All I contend therefore is that that is what he might be doing, in accordance with a quite standard intellectual practice. One cannot rule out the possibility except by assuming that what Marx intends to assert of the nature of man here is not merely its dependence, but its complete and exclusive dependence, on the ensemble of social relations – its dependence on these relations and on nothing else whatsoever. This is a more special assumption.

The vigorous form of the sentence, asserting the presupposed dependence as an identity, may be held all the same to license it. Does this assumption, then, entail the rejection of the concept of human nature? In strictest logical terms, even it does not, but in this as in a previous instance the logic alone is uninteresting. I shall not exploit it in support of my argument. Strictly, even if the nature of man depended completely on the character of the social relations, there is the possibility already mentioned that some part of that nature would persist unchanged because some features of the social relations happened not to vary. On our definition, such a part of the nature of man could properly be called a human nature. Entirely derivative, though, of the social relations, in its own right it would account for nothing and to invoke it in explanation would be otiose; an understanding of human character and conduct could be had in exclusively sociological terms. Other overtones of 'human nature' if not constancy would be missing, such as the *natural* provenance of what the term refers to, the idea that internal as well as external constraints are placed by nature on the course of human affairs. For these reasons, we may allow that if the nature of man depends completely on the ensemble of social relations, then in effect there is no human nature although formally there still may be.

Thus (a) (ii) really covers two different interpretations of Marx's sentence with substantively divergent implications. Let us distinguish them henceforth by saying, in case of strong but incomplete dependence, that: (a_1) (ii) the nature of man is *conditioned* by the ensemble of social relations; and in case of complete dependence, that: (a_2) (ii) the nature of man is *determined* by the ensemble of social relations.

(b) (i) *In its reality human nature is disclosed by the ensemble of social relations.* We eliminated (a) (i) on the grounds that it was not plausible Marx should seek to explain an invariant human make-up by reference to something historically fluid. Human nature cannot depend, in our meaning, upon changing social facts. Now, however, we are concerned with the other connection, that the ensemble of social relations, rather than explaining human nature, in some sense just discloses what it is; and no problem exists about connecting in this way what changes with what does not. There are in fact two general senses in which it might be suggested that human nature – 'in its reality'! – is revealed by, or discovered in, the ensemble of social relations. One is literal, the other ironic.

An invariant can be such, whether as structure, pattern or, merely, particular feature, and belong to what is in other respects far from constant. Just so, a social totality subject to historical alteration might incorporate, and upon examination disclose, the invariant we are interested in, human nature. Why should Marx want to assert that it is disclosed in the social totality? Perhaps in order to draw attention to the circumstance that some of the constants of which it consists are disclosed *only* there, that some aspects even of the human nature general in humankind are not visible, so to speak, in the focus with which he taxes Feuerbach, upon 'each single individual', but only on the whole terrain of the social relations. Out there, in society, is where such aspects are manifested. That is what one must study to grasp all sides of human nature. The 'reality' of the latter would in this instance connote something like its fullness. It would contrast with the abstraction in which only the one, 'inner' side is isolated, encompass the social side too. Of course, reference to society is, for Marx, at once reference to history and change, therefore reference also to human characteristics that are impermanent. But plainly here this would not contradict the postulate of a human nature. If the third sentence does state some such connection as disclosure in a literal sense, then to contradict it was not Marx's purpose. His reference to the ensemble of social relations would indicate the site that must be explored to comprehend what human nature is. It would not be an attempt to dissolve it.

Assume, however, that that reference carries ironic

intent and disclosure becomes precisely dissolution. The pedigree of the assumption is this. One can sometimes thus relate two things, the one as being disclosed by the other, when they would in general be regarded as mutually incompatible. Typically it is a means of putting the first of them in question. The human capacity for benevolence, a cynic could suggest, was revealed at Auschwitz and Dachau. The withering away of the state, a critic of Marx might say, is to be seen in the Soviet regime. 'The civilization and justice of bourgeois order', as Marx did say, apropos the response of this order to occasions of popular insurgence, at such times 'stand forth as undisguised savagery and lawless revenge'.[9] Something similar may be thought to be involved in the sixth thesis, and the social relations be supposed to reveal in *this* manner the reality of human nature. Its 'reality' would then stand not for fullness as against one-sidedness, but for an actual state of affairs unable to accommodate what the term 'human nature' putatively denotes. It would stand for the actuality as opposed to the usual associations of the idea, and the point of the opposition would be that the actuality is such as to render term and idea altogether inappropriate to it. Human nature would here be *un*real, reduced to the ensemble of social relations.

I shall for the time being do no more, with respect to this way of construing Marx's sentence, than to register something about the assumption of ironic intent. This is that it amounts to supposing that human nature and ensemble of social relations must be concepts standing in the same sort of contradictory opposition in the sixth thesis as do those, say, of justice and lawless revenge in the above-quoted statement from *The Civil War in France*. Unless they are, there would be no reason for thinking that the social relations did not, according to Marx, disclose in the straightforward sense what human nature is.

In any case, under the rubric of (b) (i) two divergent interpretations of the third sentence have again been dissociated and these I shall distinguish as follows. Where human nature is disclosed by the social totality as a real existent, I shall say that: (b_1)(I) human nature is *manifested* in the ensemble of social relations. Where the first is disclosed by the second only in an ironic sense, that is, as non-existent, I shall say that: (b_2) (i) human nature is *dissolved* in the ensemble of social relations.

(b) (ii) *In its reality the nature of man is disclosed by the ensemble of social relations*. We can be brief with this last proposition for it is unproblematic. Of the two senses of the relationship of disclosure only one is possible here since, on our definition of the nature of man, no worthwhile meaning can be attached to the idea of its being dissolved. Whatever Marx believed about the degree of variation in their character, human beings always have a character and nobody could sensibly suggest he thought otherwise. But he could be asserting the other sense of the relationship, that: (b_1) (ii) the nature of man is manifested in the ensemble of social relations. If he is, it obviously does not entail the denial of a human nature. The overall character of human beings manifested in the social relations could include this unchanging component.

From the preceding analysis we have, then, five different versions of Marx's sentence. Somewhat abbreviated, these are:

(a_1) (ii) The nature of man is socially conditioned.
(a_2) (ii) The nature of man is socially determined.
(b_1) (i)   Human nature is manifested in society.
(b_2) (i)   Human nature is dissolved in society.
(b_1) (ii) The nature of man is manifested in society.

I shall amalgamate (a_2) (ii) with (b_2) (i) as yielding broadly similar interpretations of the sixth thesis. Whether the nature of man is determined by or human nature is dissolved in the social relations, the result is that Marx in effect rejects the notion of human nature. I shall likewise amalgamate (b_1) (i) with (b_1) (ii). If human nature is manifested in society, then *ipso facto* the nature of man is too, embodying as it does whatever anthropological constants there may be; the one contention presupposes, and the other does not exclude, belief on Marx's part in the existence of a human nature, and the idea behind each is similar enough to justify considering them together.

Rearranging in this manner gives three rough alternatives which I render thus:

(1) In its reality the nature of man is conditioned by the ensemble of social relations.

(2) In its reality human nature, or the nature of man, is manifested in the ensemble of social relations.

(3) In its reality the nature of man is determined by, or human nature is dissolved in, the ensemble of social relations.

I now comment upon each of these before proceeding to argue that if Marx meant any of them he meant (1) or (2); not (3).

(1) *In its reality the nature of man is conditioned by the ensemble of social relations.* If we take Marx's third sentence in this way, it would represent, in essence, an early formulation of the central proposition of historical materialism. It would be precursor to the famous passage of the 1859 *Preface*, in which he identifies the 'totality of . . . relations of production' as foundation to the superstructure and goes on to claim that the 'mode of production of material

life conditions the general process of social, political and intellectual life'.[10] The later passage is less compressed and it is also less generic, referring to the relations of production rather than all social relations and to distinct dimensions of social, political and intellectual life rather than the nature of man overall; but there is an obvious continuity of basic idea in that the shape, loosely speaking, of human existence is held in both cases to depend upon a set of historically specific relations.

Yet, the sixth thesis would not thereby signal any 'rupture' with the supposition of a human nature. For, if the third sentence is construed as meaning (1), the dependence declared by it is not complete, the character of human beings must therefore depend on something else as well and it can be due in part to stable, natural causes. We are entitled then to put what I have called the mild interpretation on the second and last sentences. Concerned, as these obviously must be now, with the nature of man, they would be aimed only against the too one-sided focus in Feuerbach's conception of it upon general characteristics inherent in the species. Marx would be wanting, by contrast, to stress the conditioning always exercised on it by the prevailing social relations, but he would not be denying that there are general characteristics. The sixth thesis, harbinger of his mature conception of history, would involve no repudiation of human nature and would be in line with the contention of this essay that repudiation of it is no part of historical materialism.

(2) *In its reality human nature, or the nature of man, is manifested in the ensemble of social relations.* I enlarge first on the statement as it applies to the invariant entity. Its point would be to insist upon what can be termed, without paradox, human nature's social qualities. An element here

may be, indeed, that sociality as such is integral to human nature, but more than this generality can be intended.

Consider the example of language. It is a general human capacity. In the terms set by the sixth thesis, it is meaningful all the same to affirm that unlike, say, respiration, language does not exist 'in each single individual' but only in the social relationship between individuals. Although it is they that speak it and though they use it also privately, as in thought, it necessarily presupposes a social and public domain. It is a capacity whose very mode of expression is a social one, a human quality only exhibited in the manifold relations of society. None of this is to say however that, with regard to language, *nothing* is inherent in the individual, in the type of brain, for example, that is his biological endowment; or that, being a social fact, language is therefore on a par with all other social facts – monarchy, belief in miracles, inflation, the game of cricket. It is quite consistent to hold both that it has an intrinsic universality and permanence which can be put down to human *nature* and, simultaneously, that it is an ability only manifested in *society*. A similar argument can be made about Marx's own special preoccupation, material production. There is a general human capacity for it. But it requires the social framework as well as taking on collective forms, and to get a sense of what it amounts to, what it is a capacity for, one must look beyond the single individual to its results in the social and collective context: transformations wrought on the physical environment, structures erected, materials quarried or gathered, instruments made and used, products fashioned, and so on.

This could be the point of Marx's sentence then, energetic reference to the social dimensions of human nature, reference to its exoteric actuality in human society by way of complementing and not of negating the idea of intrinsic individual characteristics. The second and last sentences of the thesis, applying in this case to human nature, once again carry the sense of our mild interpretation.

So can they also, when we consider (2) in its application to the nature of man. The exoteric actuality may now be a changing rather than a common and enduring one; distinct historical modes of production, particular languages, more generally, social and cultural diversity. But the thought is basically the same, namely that, whatever it may be in the given historical circumstances, the nature of man is to be discovered in the totality of the social world. The range of human qualities and possibilities takes actual shape in the relations between individuals, so it is these relations that must be investigated if you would grasp that nature entire. That this thought refers us to a social and historical diversity in no way tells against the concept of human nature, since there is nothing in the thought to say that such diversity does not contain permanent characteristics innate in each human being.

(3) *In its reality the nature of man is determined by, or human nature is dissolved in, the ensemble of social relations.* One way or another, treated thus Marx's proposition does involve the denial of a human nature and requires that the second and final sentences of the thesis assume the meaning of our stern interpretation. Whichever they concern, whether the nature of man or human nature, they then betoken not just qualification, but rejection, of the idea of general human characteristics inherent in each individual, and we have in sum the reading of the sixth thesis that I contest.

I shall let others speak for it here. In doing so, I respect, indeed display, their own usages, and these are not identical with the ones to which I have hitherto adhered; but the want of exact terminological uniformity cannot obscure the substantive point that Marx's words are widely held to be a dismissal of the concept of human nature, in the sort of interpretation of them to be now documented.

Quoted directly or referred to, the sixth thesis has been given out as attesting that: 'Marx . . . occasionally went to the extreme of representing human nature as *merely* the manifestation in the individual of the social relations, or social institutions, of the age' (Tom Bottomore); 'Marx was beginning to dissolve individual human nature into "the ensemble of social relations" ' (Robert D. Cumming); Marx, after the early writings, 'rejects . . . specifically' the conception of a 'universal nature common to all men' or an 'essential human nature' (Eugene Kamenka); 'In 1845, Marx broke radically with every theory that based history and politics on an essence of man', and 'Marx rejected the problematic of the earlier philosophy . . . a problematic of *human nature* (or the essence of man)' which implied '(1) that there is a universal essence of man; (2) that this essence is the attribute of "*each single individual*"' (Louis Althusser); 'Marx rejects all essentialist theories, that is, all theories about human beings, society, history, which begin from characterizations of the intrinsic natures of individuals, whether such natures are conceived of in transcendental (for example Christian) or in naturalistic (for example Hobbesian) terms' (Wal Suchting); 'it was not merely the radical costume changes which, between its successive historical bows, the human genus indulged in that were irksome to Marx and Engels – it was the human genus itself' (Vernon Venable – who also writes '"human nature" . . . was for them no single universal form or general essence which individual human beings share', and 'when they do speak generally of human "nature" in any spirit other than ironic . . . it must never be understood as signifying the "absolute essence" as contrasted with the "accidents" of the human, or its permanence as contrasted with its change. Rather must it be understood as its "*history*'").[11]

Marx's thesis has been cited as signifying: the 'thoroughly "socialized" or depersonalized version of Marxism' emergent from 1845, 'a mental world from which "man" seems to be absent' (Robert Tucker); 'the denial of essentialist accounts of human nature' and 'the general truth of the non-instantiation of essence in the real' (Kate Soper); 'there is no such thing as "the essence of man" ' (Colin Sumner); 'individuals are to be regarded not as the origin or constituting basis of their relations but rather as the "bearers" of those relations' (Wal Suchting); 'man can *be* no more than what men actually do in their concrete historical and social environments' (Vernon Venable); 'No social phenomenon . . . can be explained in terms of any of the traits imputed to individuals as creatures of *nature* ', and 'If one must speak of the "essence of man", one must find it in man's civilization, material and ideal, and not in biology' (Sidney Hook).[12]

Most, though not all, of these arguments obviously go beyond a concern with the meaning of the sixth thesis, using the latter in support of a more far-reaching claim about the development of Marx's thought. In so far as this is so, one should note that it is the claim's generality, emphasized in several of the quoted passages, that gives it its point. No one could be startled if the argument were only that Marx disputed or forsook some conceptions of a universal human nature. There might be room even then for controversy over particulars, but it would be a quite different kind of contention, consistent with the recognition that *a* concept of human nature still finds its place in his mature theory of history.

To dwell briefly on this feature of the most influential

version of the claim, Althusser's: according to him, whereas pre-Marxist social theory, political economy, ethics, epistemology, all involved the 'two complementary postulates' said to be constitutive of the 'problematic of *human nature* (or the essence of man)' – that such a universal exists and that it is the attribute of each individual – and only the 'content' assigned to them varied as between different thinkers, Marx for his part 'rejected the whole of this organic system of postulates'.[13] The 'radically new concepts' of historical materialism, 'concepts of social formation, productive forces, relations of production, superstructure, ideologies',[14] do not then accommodate the concept of human nature. They are opposed to it and they supplant it. Althusser writes: 'This total theoretical revolution was only empowered to reject the old concepts because it replaced them by new concepts'; and 'Marx replaced the old couple individuals/human essence in the theory of history by new concepts (forces of production, relations of production, etc.)'.[15] It is only consistent with the conceptual dichotomy so posited that the texts of Althusserianism are strewn with such assertions, 'structuralist', sociologically reductionist, in truth historicist, in character, as that the agents of production are 'never anything more than the occupants' of places determined by the structure of the relations of production, that 'individuals are merely the effects' of the structure, that they 'are only *class representatives*', '*are nothing more than masks*', and so forth.[16]

Of course, it goes without saying that the writers I have cited are not of one mind in everything. The common way with Marx's sixth thesis just exhibited should not be taken for complete community of belief. What perhaps does not go without saying is that, where these writers elaborate on the statements quoted and especially where they support what they take to be Marx's idea, the positions they adopt are as a rule not even coherent internally. It might, on this account and their behalf, be urged that they do not 'really' hold the views I have ascribed to them; proof that they do not residing precisely in their inconsistency, in other of their statements not compatible with those reported here and indicative of more sensible assumptions. This sort of objection, however, is beside the point. For, nothing has been ascribed to anyone other than what each actually asserts. That some of the authors also ignore the consequences of the ideas asserted and contradict them, is not something which a critic *of the ideas* will, or need, feel reluctant to concede. On the contrary, it is part of the case against these ideas that their proponents are virtually bound to depart from them. The standpoint they constitute is untenable and can only be stated at the cost of some intellectual torsion, a confusion of thought or of language or both. More generally, while it may sometimes be to the credit of persons, it is then no true defence of what they say, that they do not really mean what they say.

The type of inconsistency in question, and to which I shall later return, has been frequent within Marxism. Although the theory requires, and in its parent version explicitly possesses, a concept of human nature, many Marxists try nevertheless to repress this. As has been aptly remarked, 'the slogan – literally meaningless outside the context of idealism – that "there is no such thing as human nature" has been repeated so often that it has acquired the force of a truism in Marxist circles'.[17] It can appear in unlikely places. To round off comment on (3) with just one striking instance, we may take Istvan Meszaros's book, *Marx's Theory of Alienation*. Its approach is not a 'structuralist' one. Lock, stock and barrel, its treatment of Marx turns around the idea of a human nature, as might be inferred from its very title. Yet it has for a kind of illogical refrain the emphatic denial of this. Hence, according to Meszaros, 'Marx categorically rejected the idea of a "human essence" ', and 'he does not accept such a thing as a *fixed* human nature', and 'Nothing is . . . "implanted in *human* nature" '.[18]

My dissection of the sixth thesis being, at last, concluded, I shall move on to the argument for dismissing (3) as an account of Marx's meaning. I do not say the above analysis exhausts all ways of construing these lines. Rebuttal of (3) does not require that it should. All I have done is to follow the usage just now exemplified that, in rendering 'menschliche Wesen' and generally, the term 'human nature' can be interchanged with 'the essence of man', and distinguishing then two standard senses, a narrower and a broader sense, of that term by my discrimination between 'human nature' and 'the nature of man', to explore on this basis what possibilities the text suggests. Other meanings could doubtless be proposed, or other shades of meaning. Thus the critical referent could perhaps be 'the human *being* in its actuality'. But further proposals will not affect the main contours of the argument. It is enough if it has been shown that there are, besides the line of interpretation being challenged, plausible ways of reading the thesis in which no denial of a human nature is involved. Taken so often for granted, its own evidential status is then made problematic and we are driven to other evidence to see what is the more likely in this matter.

It is not altogether eccentric to note that there are problems about the sense of the thesis, even if at such length as this it may be. Althusser himself says of the central formulation that, in strict terms, *'it means nothing at all'* and other comments of more or less Althusserian inspiration describe it similarly as strained 'to the point of incoherence', as 'enigmatic', 'merely gestural'.[19] In spite of this, the contested sense will confidently – and in these instances incongruously – be declared the import of the sixth of Marx's *Theses* without proper recourse to adjacent works and what they might indicate about his meaning. In the circumstances there are good chances that the imputation is arbitrary. To fix on a meaning without more ado, in peremptory or innocent fashion, is to risk finding in Marx's words not his thought but your own. For, the pivotal formula of the third sentence admits of more than one possible elaboration; just as a consequence of the peculiarity of it commonly noted albeit under various descriptions; just because its tense concision does present a problem. It can only be resolved in the larger semantic and intellectual context. Alone, the mere construction cannot justify these certainties about Marx's meaning.

Thus suppose I should say about history, 'In its reality it is the development of the productive forces'. What exactly would I mean? That this is all history is, or that this is in general its most important aspect, or that for the particular purpose at hand this is what is relevant or interesting about it? That history is the product of this development, or a record of it, or its mere outward form or appearance? If the statement is all you have, you do not have enough. You cannot give my exact meaning. In fact you also have, willy-nilly, a certain background to this example, given which it might be reasonable to think I was stating a familiar relation of dependence, claiming – and emphatically: in opposition to competing notions – that the development of the productive forces is what explains the course of history. Even so, how much of it would I be claiming their development explains? Some very considerable part? The broad outline? Everything? What precise degree of dependence would I, by my statement, intend? With no enlargement, you simply could not judge. You might assume that I had in mind here an exhaustive dependence, but that would be only your assumption and quite possibly mistaken.

It is the same in the present case. If Marx is asserting the dependence of the nature of man on the social relations and you just take him to mean a complete dependence, to mean in my terms that this nature is socially determined rather than socially conditioned (respectively (a$_2$) (ii) and (a$_1$) (ii) above), then you just attribute the thought to him on an inadequate basis.

Or let us say you see the reality of human nature disputed in Marx's construction through being, as I have put it, dissolved in the ensemble of social relations. But if I maintain that, contrary to some misconception or other about it, in its reality the fascist ethos *is* Auschwitz, Dachau, Treblinka, and so on, I am not thereby disputing its reality, attempting to dissolve it; as I almost certainly would be the reality of human benevolence if I so identified that. Rather, I am affirming it, by signalling in what it is to be found: its characteristic features or most notorious results or fullest expression. That Marx's formula is not affirmation but negation of human nature nevertheless, might be supposed to be entailed in the very concept of the ensemble of social relations. This is the supposition I registered when presenting (b$_2$) (i), that that concept and the idea of a human nature are incompatibly opposed. It provides a basis for ascribing to Marx the kind of ironic intent that will make his words a dissolution of human nature in the social relations rather than its association with them in some more positive sense, such as my suggestion – (b$_1$) (i) – that it is manifested in them. However, if you start with this as a supposition, you do not establish, you simply take it for granted that the historical materialist concepts in his thought exclude and replace the postulate of a human nature. You do not show that no such postulate is involved in his notion of the social whole. You presume it.

The point here is not – yet – that the content of the presumption is extraordinary. It is that, relative to this famous aphorism of Marx's, it is *merely* a presumption. Unless therefore something else from his work can be adduced in its favour, it is as arbitrary a basis as can be for determining what he means. And indeed any decision will be, one way or another, arbitrary that professes to unfold, just from the compression of that aphorism, his meaning clear and whole. The sole reliable basis for a decision lies in the wider setting of Marx's ideas. I have shown that the third sentence of the thesis can be read in divergent ways. The immediate context does not suffice to resolve its ambiguity; on the contrary, I have shown how other propositions concerning man's 'nature' there, the second and last sentences, contain ambiguities symmetrical with its own. One must look, consequently, at the evidence of other writings, first of all at those closest to the *Theses on Feuerbach*.

This I shall now do, in an effort to demonstrate in the light of them that, of the three broad meanings I have distinguished, (1) is and (2) is, but (3) is not, a plausible interpretation of Marx's sense. I adopt the following procedure. From texts adjacent to the *Theses* I indicate passages similar in tendency to (1) and (2) and which support the hypothesis that such is what Marx is saying in the sixth thesis. Although, in the nature of things, I cannot so indicate the absence of passages supporting (3), I do the next best thing, which is to attest at the same time the presence of statements that, by their use of human nature and cognate ideas, contradict (3). I go on to argue that Marx's later works confirm this general picture.

It might be objected that whatever one finds in these other writings, it will not prove beyond doubt that on *this* occasion, in the sixth thesis, Marx did not intend (3) or something like it. My response to this is that proof in such a case can only be a matter of probabilities. If two ideas, *i* and *j*, are both construable from the utterance of an author the rest of whose work points to belief in *i* and denial of *j*, it is very unlikely the utterance states *j* and, in the absence of some special and well-founded explanation, perverse to hold that it does.

And if, all the previous argument notwithstanding, someone should maintain staunchly that the sixth thesis is just not ambiguous in this way, that it plainly is a rejection of the concept of human nature . . . then so be it. What follows reduces the significance of the fact to this: that one day in the spring of 1845, in some 'notes hurriedly scribbled down for later elaboration',[20] Marx delivered himself of a freak remark, of an idea which is a departure from the mainstream of his thought and therefore has no bearing on its interpretation.

III
Human Nature
and Historical
Materialism

It is surely remarkable that so many have discerned, with the emergence of the materialist conception of history, a dismissal by Marx of the idea of human nature. *The German Ideology*, after all, setting down that celebrated conception for the first time, expressly criticizes the mistake of those who, ignoring what it terms the 'real basis of history', thereby exclude from the historical process 'the relation of man to nature', create an 'antithesis of nature and history'.[21] It might be thought that, for Marx, this antithesis is mistaken only with respect to external nature, and not also with respect to nature as something inherent in humanity. But it is easy to show that this is not the case. Marx includes such an inner, human nature squarely within the 'real basis of history'.

In fact, *The German Ideology* at one point echoes a passage from *The Holy Family* just in emphasizing nature's internal as well as external dimensions. In both works, the intent behind the emphasis is a materialist one, a 'double' natural constraint being insisted upon in opposition to themes which are manifestly idealist. In *The Holy Family*, Marx accuses Bruno Bauer of sublimating 'all that affirms a *finite* material existence *outside infinite self-consciousness*' and, hence, of combating nature – 'nature both as it exists *outside* man and as man's nature'. Bauer, Marx also says, does not recognize 'any *power of human nature* distinct from *reason*'.[22] In the passage from *The German Ideology,* it is Christianity, rather, that is the object of criticism: 'The only reason why Christianity wanted to free us from the domination of the flesh and "desires as a driving force" was because it regarded our flesh, our desires as something foreign to us; it wanted to free us from determination by nature only because it regarded our own nature as not belonging to us. For if I myself am not nature, if my natural desires, my whole natural character, do not belong to myself – and this is the doctrine of Christianity – then all determination by nature – whether due to my own natural character or to what is known as external nature – seems to me a determination by something foreign, a fetter, compulsion used against me, *heteronomy as opposed to autonomy of the spirit* . . . Christianity has indeed never succeeded in freeing us from the domination of desires. . .'[23]

The resemblance between the passages is striking enough not to have to be laboured. Affirming certain natural determinants, both exploit the same linguistic device, separating nature as a whole into what is external to man and man's own. Both thereby refer to a 'nature' human beings possess in virtue precisely of nature, not of the 'particular form of society'; thus to a make-up that, relative to particular social forms, is enduring and general, a human nature in our sense. As we shall see, this sort of materialist usage of it – of 'power(s) of human nature', 'natural desires' (more often: 'needs'), 'natural character' – plays an important, *explanatory* role in the formulation of Marx's theory of history.

However, *The Holy Family* is also echoed by *The German Ideology* in a second, *normative* usage of the same idea. In some familiar lines from the former of these works,

Marx had spoken of the proletariat's indignation at its abasement, 'an indignation to which it is necessarily driven by the contradiction between its human *nature* and its condition of life'.[24] *The German Ideology* describes the proletarian similarly: as one 'who is not in a position to satisfy even the needs that he has in common with all human beings'; one whose 'position does not even allow him to satisfy the needs arising directly from his human nature'.[25] For the way in which they conflict with the needs of a common human nature, the social relations responsible for the proletarian position and condition are here implicitly condemned.

These similarities in the two works may serve to give us our bearings. In the sequence of Marx's writings, the *Theses on Feuerbach* come between *The Holy Family*, composed in late 1844, and *The German Ideology,* begun during the autumn of 1845 and discontinued the following summer. *The Holy Family* is an 'early' work; in other words, it antedates historical materialism. That it makes reference to human nature will surprise no one, since it is well-known that the concept is to be found in Marx's early writings. *The German Ideology*, on the other hand, itself proposes the theory of historical materialism. Whether or not the virtually identical references that it makes to human nature surprise anyone, they are *prima facie* testimony to a continuity of thought exactly where the sixth thesis is alleged to mark a rupture.

The German Ideology, like the *Theses*, remained unpublished during Marx's lifetime, but too much should not be made of this. For two years he and Engels tried hard to get it published, and failed.[26] Although in the event not completed, then depleted by the criticism of the mice and other vicissitudes, it is the most reliable guide we have to the ideas its authors at this time wished to put forth. If a clue is

needed to difficulties in the *Theses*, it is as likely as anything is to provide one since, written only shortly after
them, it manifestly shares and enlarges upon their preoccupations, its most interesting and important section being
given over partly to critical remarks about Feuerbach. Of
course, this work is only an initial, hence somewhat rough,
statement of historical materialism. But it is more relevant
than anything written later to deciphering the meaning of
the sixth thesis, and we shall be able to see in any case how
things stand with Marx's subsequent works.

In *The German Ideology*, as well as the similarities with
The Holy Family just observed, we find indeed the crux of
the present question. Let us examine one passage, the best
known amongst several like it and occurring, be it noted,
not just in the same work as, but right in the thick of, the
presentation of Marx's new conception of history. There is
a formulation in it that is nearly identical in character to the
central formulation of the sixth thesis. Where this one dif-
fers from that, however, is in being implanted within a
context better indicative of what it might, and also of what
it cannot, mean. 'This mode of production must not be
considered simply as being the reproduction of the physical existence of the individuals. Rather it is a definite form
of activity of these individuals, a definite form of expressing their life, a definite *mode of life* on their part. As individuals express their life, so they are. What they are, therefore, coincides with their production, both with *what* they
produce and with *how* they produce. Hence what individuals are depends on the material conditions of their
production.'[27]

The mode of production is said here to be the form in
which individuals express their life, which form is said in
turn to bear intimately on what they are. What individuals
are is declared, in consequence, to coincide with their
mode of production, and it is this, the penultimate state-

ment of the passage that is the crucial one. Despite the terminological variation, its tendency is substantially the same as that of the third sentence of the thesis. Obviously, 'what individuals are' is quite near, in the entity it denotes, to their 'nature', and that it is stated in this case to coincide with, rather than just be, the mode of production is itself a difference of little significance. Whether we have that what individuals are *coincides with*[28] their mode of production or that man's 'nature' *is* the ensemble of social relations, either way we have a relationship that is very close but whose content is otherwise somewhat vague, in need of clearer definition. In fact these are only two of a whole family of similar formulations that Marx was disposed to use at about this time. I shall introduce further of its members in due course.

In the present instance, we find clues to what the formulation might mean in its immediate context. Just before it, there is the idea that in the mode of production individuals express their life in a certain way and, according as they do so, what they are. Perhaps the penultimate sentence here is meant only to round off what has gone before, affirming such a relation of expression between mode of production and what individuals are. It would then resemble (2) above, that man's 'nature' is manifested in the ensemble of social relations. Alternatively, perhaps its meaning is explicated in what directly follows it, the assertion of a relation of dependence. On that assumption, if we take the dependence – of what individuals are upon the conditions of production – as being anything short of a total and exclusive one, then we have an idea similar to (1) above, that the nature of man is conditioned by the social relations. With neither suggestion would the formulation under scrutiny evidence any rejection of a human nature.

However, *could* Marx plausibly be thought to have

intended it as a rejection? Whether because he meant by it to reduce what individuals are to their mode of production, or because he did indeed have in mind a relation of total dependence, or whatever? Could he, *here*, be taken as having meant something like (3)? No, he could not. He could not, because in the very same place in this work, as direct preamble to the quoted passage, use is made of precisely a concept of human nature. Not only that; this use shows it to be fundamental rather than incidental to the historical conception being proposed. It is fundamental to historical materialism in the exact sense of being a part of its theoretical foundation.

What precedes the excerpt I have already quoted is this: 'The first premise of all human history is, of course, the existence of living human individuals. Thus the first fact to be established is *the physical organization of these individuals* and their consequent relation to the rest of nature. Of course, we cannot here go either into *the actual physical nature of man*, or into the natural conditions in which man finds himself – geological, oro-hydrographical, climatic and so on. *All historical writing must set out from these natural bases* and their modification in the course of history through the action of men.'[29] Italics in this passage are mine but notice the emphasis that is original to it: the 'first' fact to be established; again, one of the natural 'bases' from which historical research must 'set out' – man's physical constitution. Then, lest anyone should think to dissipate what is so plainly given here as point of departure, by leaning on the last phrase about its 'modification', the text at once goes on to associate with this basic physical make-up a quite general human attribute, an attribute, indeed, cited by Marx as specifically, distinctively human: 'Men can be distinguished from animals by consciousness, by religion or anything else you like. They themselves begin to distinguish themselves from animals as soon as they begin to *produce* their means of subsistence, a step which is conditioned by their physical organization.'[30] Only after this – a notion of human nature if such there be – do we come to the congruence we have just now seen asserted between what individuals are and a particular *mode* of production.

The identical pattern of thought is found in more compressed form at other points in *The German Ideology*. Also right in the midst of the exposition of historical materialism, there is Marx's observation, 'Men have history because they must *produce* their life, and because they must produce it moreover in a *certain* way: this is determined by their physical organization; their consciousness is determined in just the same way.' I shall digress for a moment to comment that since, hard by in the text, consciousness is identified thus with language: 'Language is as old as consciousness, language *is* practical, real consciousness that exists for other men as well, and only therefore does it also exist for me';[31] we have confirmation of the hypothesis, formulated earlier apropos of language, that Marx could perfectly well have recognized certain capacities as inherent in the natural constitution of the individual whilst urging in the strongest terms the social dimension of them. Now, let us articulate the pattern of thought ascertained. It may be put as follows: if diversity in the character of human beings is in large measure set down by Marx to historical variation in their social relations of production, the very fact that they entertain this sort of relations, the fact that they produce and that they have a history, he explains in turn by some of their general and constant, intrinsic, constitutional characteristics; in short by their human nature. This concept is therefore indispensable to his historical theory. It contributes to founding what he gives out in the theory as the material basis of society and history. To reformulate the point in the terms that have been used throughout this essay: if the nature of man depends upon the ensemble of social relations, it does not depend wholly on them, it is conditioned but not determined by them, because they themselves depend on, that is, are partly explained by human nature, which is a component of the nature of man.

One further example of this train of thought before we proceed. Elsewhere Marx again alludes to those powers of human beings that are distinctively human, in saying that 'the production, as well as the satisfaction, of [their] needs is an historical process, which is not found in the case of a sheep or a dog.' At the same place, in the sequel to this, he goes on in a vein now surely familiar: 'The conditions under which individuals have intercourse with each other . . . are conditions appertaining to their individuality, in no way external to them; conditions under which alone these definite individuals, living under definite relations, can produce their material life and what is connected with it, are thus the conditions of their self-activity and are produced by this self-activity. The definite condition under which they produce thus corresponds . . . to the reality of their conditioned nature, their one-sided existence . . .'[32] Observe the form of the last assertion. Before we had coincidence, now we have correspondence, between the actuality of individuals and the conditions of their production. Here as there, the context licenses the interpretation that the character of individuals is conditioned by the latter; it might, perhaps, license the interpretation that in the conditions of production – these being for their part 'produced by this self-activity' of the individuals – their character is in some sort manifested. However, here as there, there can be no excuse for reading the formula as a reductionist one, dismissive of human nature.

In the way of an anthropology implicated in Marx's materialist conception, we have so far encountered the idea of general human capacities or powers: in the first place that of production, but also language, as embodying human consciousness. *The German Ideology* also contains much about individuals' needs. These it explicitly assimilates at one point to their 'nature', when it states that 'their *needs, consequently their nature*, and the method of satisfying their needs' have always bound them into relations with one another.[33] It would be consistent with the argument of this essay concerning an innate human nature if Marx, then, had something to say about universal or permanent human needs, and so he does. Once more the foundational character of it is as clear as can be. Beyond those needs implicit in the statement just mentioned, namely, sexual, under the rubric 'relations between the sexes', and the social one itself – as it is expressed elsewhere, 'the need, the necessity, of intercourse with other men', 'that men need and *always have needed* each other'[34] – there is also this, in a recurring phrase 'first premise . . . of all history': 'Men must be in a position to live in order to be able to "make history". But life involves before everything else eating and drinking, housing, clothing and various other things. The first historical act is thus the production of the means to satisfy these needs, the production of material life itself. And indeed this is an historical act, a fundamental condition of all history, which today, as thousands of years ago, must daily and hourly be fulfilled merely in order to sustain human life. . . Therefore in any conception of history one has first of all to observe this fundamental fact in all its significance and all its implications and to accord it its due importance.' The Germans, so we are told, have not done this but the French and the English have begun to, to give historiography 'a materialistic basis' in the first histories of civil society and industry.[35]

So we see what putting the study of history on a 'materialistic basis' here connotes: not 'anthropology's theoretical pretensions . . . shattered'[36] and so forth, but taking fully into account the enduring imperative of essential human needs. As if the point were still wanting in emphasis, Marx afterwards reiterates that responding to this imperative is, together with the creation of new needs and the propagation of the species, one of 'three aspects of social activity . . . which have existed simultaneously since the dawn of history and the first men, and which still assert themselves in history today'.[37] Much the same idea is encompassed also in the reference, at another place, to 'desires which exist under all relations, and only change their form and direction under different social relations', the sex instinct and need to eat being cited in this connection; as contrasted with 'those originating solely in a particular society, under particular conditions of [production] and intercourse'.[38]

Essential human needs fulfil not just a theoretical function in the argument of *The German Ideology*, explanatory along with man's general powers of the productive infrastructure of human society. As befits Marx's revolutionary standpoint, they possess an overtly practical implication too, serving as a norm of judgment and of action. Thus, for example, the same needs as figure in elaborating the aforesaid first premise of all history figure equally as preconditions of human liberation. Dismissing speculative notions of this, Marx writes, '. . . it is possible to achieve real liberation only in the real world and by real means. . . in general, people cannot be liberated as long as they are unable to obtain food and drink, housing and clothing in adequate quality and quantity.'[39] Similarly, the necessity of social revolution is justified in the light of basic human needs in the following stricture which is directed specifically at Feuerbach: 'He gives no criticism of the present conditions of life. Thus he never manages to conceive the sensuous world as the total living sensuous *activity* of the individuals composing it; therefore when, for example, he sees instead of healthy men a crowd of scrofulous, over-worked and consumptive starvelings, he is compelled to take refuge in the "higher perception" and in the ideal "compensation in the species", and thus to relapse into idealism at the very point where the communist materialist sees the necessity, and at the same time the condition, of a transformation both of industry and of the social struc-ture.'[40]

Instead of healthy men . . . people whose need for rest and need for food are insufficiently met, their health wanting. This is in line with the normative usage of human nature already attested, adverse judgment upon social conditions which fail the very needs common and intrinsic to human-kind, adverse because they fail them. Noticeable in the excerpt, moreover, is a certain kinship with the *Theses on Feuerbach*. Its second assertion descends directly from both the first and the fifth of them, whilst the initial sentence is a clear echo of something in the sixth thesis itself. But the relationship is closer still than that and more relevant to our present concern. For, just prior to the lines quoted, Feuerbach is criticized in these terms, cognate beyond all possible doubt or cavil with the matter of the sixth and the seventh theses: '. . . because he still remains in the realm of theory and conceives of men not in their given social con-nection, not under their existing conditions of life, which have made them *what* they are, he never arrives at the actually existing, active men, but stops at the abstraction "man". . .'[41] As it is their social conditions, according to this, that make men what they are, it too might have been seen perhaps as evidence of a denial of human nature.

Only, we know from the sequel that what they have made them in the particular case is sick, and also overworked and hungry, all of which evokes needs that human beings do not owe to 'their given social connection' but merely to their natural constitution as human beings, even if they do owe it to the former that these needs are not more amply satisfied.

We must conclude that the 'making' in question here is conditioning, in our sense, of the nature of man; that the above criticism of Feuerbach is the mild one and not the stern, qualification not rejection of the postulate of an inherent human make-up; that it is criticism only for treating this in isolation from the effects worked on man by the given historical milieu (hence: he *stops at* the abstraction 'man'). We may take note also of the conception: the sensuous world *as* the sensuous activity of the individuals composing it; which may be suggested to resemble at least somewhat that of man's 'nature' as manifested in the ensemble of social relations. And as such are Marx's meanings in this passage on Feuerbach, it seems probable that such too was his intent in the sixth thesis, so obviously related to it. I submit in any case that this is getting to look ever more probable than interpretation (3).

If, out of everything either stated or implied by Marx in this connection, we now make a schedule of general human needs, then so far we have these: for other human beings, for sexual relations, for food, water, clothing, shelter, rest and, more generally, for circumstances that are conducive to physical health rather than disease. There is another one to be added to them before we leave *The German Ideology*, the need of people for a breadth and diversity of pursuit and hence of personal development, as Marx himself expresses these, 'all-round activity', 'all-round development of individuals', 'free development of individuals', 'the means of cultivating [one's] gifts in all directions', and so on.[42] Some will doubtless want to contest the generality of such a need. However, it is there in the work irrespective of anyone's assessment of it and my purpose for the moment is only exegesis. Marx does not, of course, take it to be a need of survival, as for example nourishment is. But then, besides considering the survival needs common to all human existence, he is sensible also, as we have already seen, of the requirements of 'healthy' human beings and of what is 'adequate' for 'liberated' ones; he speaks too of conditions that will allow a 'normal' satisfaction of needs.[43] These epithets plainly show that, for all his well-known emphasis on the historical variability of human needs, he still conceives the variation as falling within some limits and those not just the limits of a bare subsistence. Even above subsistence level, too meagre provision for, equally repression of, certain common needs will be the cause of one kind and degree of *suffering* or another: illness or disability, malnutrition, physical pain, relentless monotony and exhaustion, unhappiness, despair. The requirement, as Marx sees it, for variety of activity has to be understood in this sense, precondition not of existence as such but of a fulfilled or satisfying, a joyful, one.

Just see how he talks about neglect of the need in question. He talks of 'subjection of the individual under the division of labour' and of an exclusive sphere of activity as 'forced upon him';[44] of labour as 'unbearable' for the worker, deprived of 'all semblance of self-activity' and, again, 'forced upon him';[45] of the worker himself as 'sacrificed from youth onwards'.[46] Labour is said only to sustain the life of individuals 'by stunting it' and the existing social relations to be responsible for 'crippling' them[47] – a 'physical, intellectual and social crippling and enslavement' this, one of whose aspects is the 'suppression' of artistic talent in most people as a consequence of the division of labour.[48] Throughout history hitherto, according to Marx, 'some persons satisfied their needs at the expense of others, and therefore some – the minority – obtained the monopoly of development, while others – the majority – owing to the constant struggle to satisfy their most essential needs, were for the time being (i.e., until the creation of new revolutionary productive forces) excluded from any development.'[49] This is not the language of a belief that the nature of man depends simply upon the historically given form of society but a language of some tension between them, and its premise, manifestly, the frustration of enduring human needs.

That ends my argument from *The German Ideology*. We have seen there: explicit references to a human nature; usage of the concept that is integral to Marx's new theory of history, being of a fundamental explanatory kind; usage equally of a normative kind; and some part of the substance of his idea of human nature, certain general human characteristics, both capacities and needs. We have seen, moreover, passages bearing a resemblance to the sixth thesis, and I have tried to show that they support my interpretation (1) and maybe also (2) but nowise the contested interpretation, (3). Having begun thus by going forward in time from the *Theses on Feuerbach*, I want next to go back from them, to things written just the year before. This may sound at first to be a rather pointless exercise, since those who contend Marx broke with all idea of a human nature generally locate the break from 1845 onwards. In the circumstances, what could writings of 1844 possibly disclose? They disclose in fact matter of the greatest relevance: a veritable *reductio ad absurdum* of the tradition that the concise central formula of the sixth thesis – of all things, Marx's formula associating man's 'nature' with the ensemble of social relations – is proof and expression of that conceptual break.

For the truth is that the passages which are closest to this laconic affirmation, which most resemble it in form, inflection, emphasis, these passages actually predate it. They belong precisely to Marx's early writings. We encountered in *The German Ideology* assertions to the effect that what individuals are, their reality, *coincides* or *corresponds* with their mode, or with their conditions, of production, or else is what their conditions have *made* them; and I proposed a substantial similarity between this sort of assertion and the third sentence of the thesis. In earlier texts, however, the similarity of substance is complemented by an identity of form as Marx puts forward, exactly in the manner of the sixth thesis, that now man, now man's 'nature', now the individual simply *is* society or the community or the social whole. To claim of the passages in which he does this that *they* are denials of human nature would be absurdity indeed. For one thing, they wear it upon their face that they are not. For another, which is explanation of the first, they coexist with the entire conception of human nature known to pervade the early writings, sitting cheek by jowl with ideas of alienation and human emancipation that depend on it. In exhibiting these several passages, I call attention yet again to the support that is provided for (1) and (2) as ways of construing the sixth thesis.

The first of them is from the *Contribution to the Critique of Hegel's Philosophy of Right. Introduction:* 'Man makes *religion*, religion does not make man. Religion is the self-consciousness and self-esteem of man who has either not yet found himself or has already lost himself again. But *man* is no abstract being encamped outside the world. Man is *the world of man*, the state, society. This state, this society, produce religion, an *inverted world-consciousness*, because they are an *inverted world*.'[50] The point of departure, as in the sixth thesis, is religion and it is stated, as in the seventh, to be a social product. One and the same context therefore, and lo and behold: *But man is no abstract being* (Wesen) . . . *Man is the world of man . . . society* – one and the same thought as well beyond any question. The reminder is perhaps appropriate that it is in this *Introduction* that Marx makes the following, somewhat 'humanist' declaration: 'To be radical is to grasp the root of the matter. But for man the root is man himself. . . The criticism of religion ends . . . with the *categorical imperative to overthrow all relations* in which man is a debased, enslaved, forsaken, despicable being.'[51]

Now here is an extract from Marx's Paris notebooks, from his *Comments on James Mill*: 'Since *human* nature is the *true community* of men, by manifesting their *nature* men *create*, produce, the *human community*, the social entity, which is no abstract universal power opposed to the single individual, but is the essential nature of each individual, his own activity, his own life, his own spirit, his own wealth.'

A few lines further on, it is said again of this community: 'Men, not as an abstraction, but as real, living, particular individuals, *are* this entity. Hence, *as* they are, so is this entity itself.'

And shortly after that, there is reference to: 'The *community of men*, or the manifestation of the nature of *men*, their mutual complementing the result of which is species-life. . .'[52] Thus, man's 'nature' and the social entity are identified repeatedly, with the former, quite explicitly here, held to be *manifested* in the latter.

The themes of these excerpts from Marx's notebooks then recur in the *Economic and Philosophical Manuscripts*. One passage there distinctly echoes the first excerpt:

'Above all we must avoid postulating "society" again as an abstraction *vis-à-vis* the individual. The individual *is the social being*. His manifestations of life – even if they may not appear in the direct form of *communal* manifestations of life carried out in association with others – *are* therefore an expression and confirmation of *social life*.'

What follows recalls, in turn, the second one: 'Man, much as he may therefore be a *particular* individual (and it is precisely his particularity which makes him an individual, and a real *individual* social being), is just as much the *totality*.'[53]

It so happens, in other words, that this type of formulation comes very freely from Marx's pen before 1845 and evidently without signifying renunciation of the idea of human nature. What reason, then, is there for thinking that exactly the same type of formulation suddenly becomes, in the *Theses on Feuerbach*, the expression of just such a renunciation? There is an argument due to Althusser which might be offered in response to the question but it fails here. It is that every theoretical element – formula, assertion or concept – takes its significance only from the wider conceptual field which it inhabits. Within two different 'problematics', elements that are ostensibly similar may diverge in meaning. However, for this reasoning to be applicable in the present case, it is not enough that, as is demonstrable, a new theory emerges in Marx's work from 1845. In addition we must already know the theory to contain material permitting the inference that he now dispenses with assumptions of human nature. But as things stand, we do not *already* know this. It is what is in question.

Marx's characterization of man's 'nature' in the sixth thesis is itself supposed to be the evidence for it, remember. Once we have shown what poor evidence that is by displaying its continuity with a group of similar formulations in the early writings, mere gesturing towards the notion of the 'problematic' cannot restore its credentials. It would require something rather more cogent, substantive evidence *from* the wider conceptual context, to establish that this apparent continuity is actually a discontinuity and a species of assertion hitherto perfectly compatible with the assumption of a human nature now contradicts it flatly. The wider context of Marx's famous characterization of man's 'nature' is formed, in the first instance, only by a few brief notes, the rest of the *Theses on Feuerbach*. There is nothing in them that could prove there has been this abrupt change of meaning. And we have already seen what happens when we look further afield to the work that directly follows. We are left, therefore, with a nice irony, in the circumstances of this discussion: the formula cited with such facility and frequency as revealing Marx's repudiation of his youthful belief in the existence of a human nature has the clearest possible pedigree precisely in the writings of his youth.

I have no quarrel, incidentally, with the view that the developments which do occur in Marx's thought around 1845 are of a decisive importance. The theoretical ensemble that begins to take shape then, by tradition 'historical materialism', outweighs in intellectual fertility and power, as well as in its political consequence, the content of the early writings. Althusser's proposal of the *epistemological break* had the merit of focusing upon this when it needed emphasis, in face of a widespread tendency to promote the early at the expense of the later writings, a Marxist ethic at the expense of Marx's theory, his humanism at the expense of his scientific and political achievement. However, nobody is obliged by the alternative simplicities, 'One Marx or two?' The real picture is of a theoretical development marked in places by genuine novelty and change, but marked equally by some stability of conception, by definite continuities and strong ones. Its details are amenable to careful study. Besides rendering a worthwhile service, the epistemological break also carried with it a lot of excess doctrinal baggage and some bad intellectual habits. A whole obscurantism of the 'problematic' enabled the discovery in Marx of concepts, novelties – the latest Parisian fashions – positions, discontinuities, that simply are not there. Amongst such 'absent presences' is his alleged break with every general anthropology. In truth, there is a continuity here: he subscribed to the supposition of a common human nature from beginning to end. I finish the demonstration of this by moving now beyond the immediate textual environment of the *Theses* to works of a later period.

The products of Marx's maturity, in particular *Capital* and the writings most closely related to it, provide ample reinforcement of virtually everything that has been set out above. It would be tedious and is unnecessary to go through it at length. My case is in essence already made, the rebuttal of (3) as an interpretation of the sixth thesis having deprived the standpoint which I contest of its only presentable support. At this stage, it will be sufficient if we just confirm that the broad lines of what has been established run on into Marx's subsequent works.

To begin with, there is still the overt talk of a human nature in our sense. One instance of it, part of some unfavourable comment on Jeremy Bentham, is the following: 'To know what is useful for a dog, one must investigate the nature of dogs. This nature is not itself deducible from the principle of utility. Applying this to man, he that would judge all human acts, movements, relations, etc. according to the principle of utility would first have to deal with human nature in general, and then with human nature as historically modified in each epoch. Bentham does not trouble himself with this. With the dryest naiveté he assumes that the modern petty bourgeois, especially the English petty bourgeois, is the normal man.'[54] It could be no clearer surely, a distinction pretty well matching the one used here throughout and Bentham accused in the light of it, but of generalizing arbitrarily and not for the idea itself of a general human nature; accused indeed of failure to explore what human nature is in a serious way. A second instance – the normative usage this time – concerns Marx's distinction between the realm of necessity and the realm of freedom. Referring to the former, the sphere of material production, he writes: 'Freedom in this field can only consist in socialized man, the associated producers, rationally regulating their interchange with nature, bringing it under their common control, instead of being ruled by it as by the blind forces of nature; and achieving this with the least expenditure of energy and under conditions most favourable to, and worthy of, their human nature.'[55]

Another instance involves the division within nature that we encountered earlier. Marx speaks of wealth, stripped of its bourgeois form, as the 'full development of human mastery over the forces of nature, those of so-called nature as well as of humanity's own nature'; and he links this to something else we have already encountered, namely, the 'absolute working-out of [man's] creative potentialities', with 'the development of all human powers as such the end in itself'.[56] The same idea recurs in a defence of Ricardo: 'production for its own sake means nothing but the development of human productive forces, in other words the *development of the richness of human nature as an end in itself*'.[57] And by contrast there is repeated allusion to this 'nature', seat of potentialities and powers, as setting also certain natural *limits* – on the productivity of labour, on the length of the working day, at the lower end of the value of labour-power.[58]

Besides references to human nature of a direct kind, all the complementary theoretical matter gathered from *The German Ideology* also persists. If there is no longer any exact counterpart of the type of formulation exemplified by the third sentence of the sixth thesis and with which the writings close to the *Theses* are replete, there is still, time and again, the assertion of at least a part of its central point. The human being is a social being, 'not merely a gregarious animal, but an animal which can individuate itself only in the midst of society'.[59] It is not uncommon, of course, to treat this very insistence upon man's sociality, in historicist fashion, as repelling any assumption of a human uniformity. But that is the simplest of logical errors. Whatever degree of historical variation the thought may imply, it is itself a *generalization about human nature*. As a caution against historicist responses to it, it is worth drawing attention to a visibly naturalist, some will doubtless say even 'vulgar materialist', dimension of this thought. In the chapter on 'Co-operation' in *Capital*, Marx puts forward the view: 'Apart from the new power that arises from the fusion of many forces into a single force, mere social contact begets in most industries a rivalry and a stimulation of the "animal spirits", which heightens the efficiency of each individual worker. . . This originates from the fact that man, if not as Aristotle thought a political animal, is at all events a social animal.'[60] A little further on, he repeats this – that the combination of individuals 'raises their animal spirits' – as one amongst several aspects of 'the productive power of social labour', of the fact that the worker, co-operating with others, 'strips off the fetters of his individuality, and develops the capabilities of his species'.[61]

Amongst such capabilities of the human species, the first

place in Marx's interest continues to be occupied by production. It is a human universal, its universality expressed in terms both of possibility and of necessity. As possibility, it is labour-power, 'the labour-power possessed in his bodily organism by every ordinary man', 'the aggregate of those mental and physical capabilities existing in the physical form, the living personality, of a human being'.[62] These, 'the natural forces which belong to his own body, his arms, legs, head and hands',[63] man sets in motion in the labour process and the labour process is itself a necessity. It is 'a condition of human existence which is independent of all forms of society; it is an eternal natural necessity which mediates the metabolism between man and nature, and therefore human life itself'.[64] It is, again, 'the universal condition for the metabolic interaction between man and nature . . . common to all forms of society in which human beings live'.[65] And it distinguishes the species. 'We presuppose labour,' Marx writes, 'in a form in which it is an exclusively human characteristic' and, contrasting it with 'those first instinctive forms of labour which remain on the animal level', he emphasizes, in the famous comparison of the architect and the bee, its purposiveness or intentionality, the conscious regulation of the mode of activity according to ends that are conceived in advance.[66] Equally, the 'use and construction of instruments of labour, although present in germ among certain species of animals, is characteristic of the specifically human labour process'.[67] The elements of this process, materials, instruments and the worker's activity, Marx describes as 'immutable natural conditions' and 'absolute determinations of *human* labour as such, as soon as it has evolved beyond the purely animal'.[68]

What we find in the later writings with respect to this human power, the faculty of production, we find also with respect to man's needs – confirmation of the position previously expounded. There is the same conceptual conjunction that was noted in *The German Ideology*, in the form now, 'my needs . . . my own nature, this totality of needs and drives',[69] and consonant with our case that for Marx the individual's 'nature' incorporates a constant, a human nature as defined, there are needs once more of a permanent and general kind. They appear under various headings, 'natural needs', 'physically indispensable means of subsistence', 'physical needs', on the one hand; but also 'social requirements', on the other.[70] To be sure, the first sort are said to vary with climatic and other circumstances and the second to be conditioned by the 'level of civilization'. Yet a certain generality of needs remains intact for all that, and as before we may make a schedule of them, this one a little more elaborate than the first: food, clothing, shelter, fuel, rest and sleep; hygiene, 'healthy maintenance of the body', fresh air and sunlight; intellectual requirements, social intercourse, sexual needs in so far as they are presupposed by 'relations between the sexes'; the needs of support specific to infancy, old age and incapacity, and the need for a safe and healthy working environment ('space, light, air and protection against the dangerous or the unhealthy concomitants of the production process' – otherwise the 'five senses . . . pay the penalty').[71]

Such needs determine the universal 'metabolism' between man and nature and constitute an element in the value of labour-power; they establish the upper limit on the length of the working day and account for the portion of surplus labour which must always be performed on behalf of those incapable of working. In addition, however, to what they are called upon by Marx to explain, their normative function in his mature work is as prominent as ever. Whatever else it is, theory and socio-historical explanation, and scientific as it may be, that work is a moral indictment resting on a conception of essential human needs, an ethical standpoint, in other words, in which a view of human nature is involved. Is it really possible to doubt or overlook this in face of the clear, persistent, passionate discourse of *Capital*? We read there of the 'horrors' and the 'torture' and the 'brutality' of overwork;[72] of capital's 'robbery' and 'theft', within the labour process, of the most elementary prerequisites of the worker's health, 'the absence of all provisions to render the production process human, agreeable or at least bearable';[73] that the search for economy here is 'murderous' – hence of industrial 'horrors' surpassing those in Dante's Inferno – and that capital also 'usurps' and 'steals' the time for meeting other vital needs,[74] and of 'necessities of life' insufficient to satisfy the mass of the people 'decently and humanely', 'overcrowded habitations, absolutely unfit for human beings', 'vile housing conditions', 'accumulation of misery', 'physical and mental degradation'.[75] We read of capital's lack of concern for the 'normal maintenance' of labour-power, of concern solely for its maximum expenditure, 'no matter how diseased, compulsory and painful it may be';[76] of a 'shameless squandering', a 'reckless squandering', a 'laying waste and debilitating' of labour-power, a laying waste thereby of 'the natural force of human beings';[77] and of 'the prodigious dissipation of the labourer's life and health' by a mode of production 'altogether too prodigal with its human material'.[78] Marx describes the lot of the workers as requiring 'ceaseless human sacrifices' and as a 'martyrology'.[79] The increase of wealth under capitalism he describes as being brought about 'at the expense of the individual human being'.[80]

Extant amongst his preoccupations, finally, is 'the worker's own need for development': therefore the time available for 'the free play of the vital forces of his body and his mind'; '*scope* for the development of man's faculties'; and a variety of pursuit – for 'a man's vital forces . . . find recreation and delight,' Marx says, in 'change of activity'.[81] Of course, time, scope and variety do not necessarily mean the absence of all effort and are not in fact proposed by him in that sense. The expenditure of labour-power, he contends, is 'man's normal life-activity', some work and 'suspension of tranquillity' a need, the 'overcoming of obstacles . . . a liberating activity'. Genuinely free work can require 'the most intense exertion'.[82] However, this is self-determining exertion and conceived as part of a breadth of individual development. From the *Communist Manifesto*, with its well-known phrase concerning 'the free development of each' and 'the free development of all', to the *Critique of the Gotha Programme*, which canvasses 'the all-round development of the individual',[83] that preoccupation of Marx's is manifested in writings of directly programmatic import and, as for his theoretical writings, they are fairly strewn with the signs of it: 'artistic, scientific etc. development' and 'full development' and 'free intellectual and social activity' of the individual;[84] 'free activity . . . not dominated by the pressure of an extraneous purpose' and 'that development of human energy which is an end in itself',[85] 'a society in which the full and free development of every individual forms the ruling principle' and an education, correspondingly, of 'fully developed human beings'.[86] In these expressions and others like them, Marx envisages a better life for human beings. Simultaneously, in a language and imagery of suffering, oppression, incompletion and impairment, he seeks to depict a long and ongoing experience of deficiency, one more category of unfulfilled human need. Thus, exploited and externally imposed, labour is 'repulsive', a 'torment', 'slavery'.[87] In the capitalist division of labour, 'hideous' or 'monstrous' in its forms,[88] the worker is 'annexed for life by a limited function' – a single faculty developed 'at the expense of all others' – 'crippled . . . through the suppression of a whole world of productive drives and inclinations', crippled in 'body and mind' and attacked 'at the very roots of his life', 'bound hand and foot for life to a single specialized operation', 'riveted to the most simple manipulations'.[89] There is a 'suppression of his individual vitality, freedom and autonomy' and of 'the many-sided play of the muscles'.[90] Transformed from an early age into a 'mere machine for the production of surplus-value', or having to be 'a part of a specialized machine', a 'living appendage' of it, the worker is distorted – into 'a fragment of a man'.[91]

IV
For Human Nature

The evidence is clear and abundant. Marx did not reject the idea of a human nature. It remains only to consider how the misconception can be so common that he did. Apart from the sixth thesis itself, two rather different sets of reasons, none of them adequate, are mobilized to sustain it: first, what purports to be other textual evidence in its favour (and thus counter to that assembled above); second, considerations as to why the concept of human nature *should* be rejected. Strictly speaking, considerations of this second kind are irrelevant to the case, but we may examine them all the same. I now briefly review and criticize the several reasons, of both kinds, one by one.

As to the other textual evidence, it consists of arguments of Marx's supposed, just like the thesis, to prove a denial of human nature on his part. In the role of proof, however, these arguments are worth even less than the thesis is. In different ways, they have reference to man and to concepts of man, that is all. The evidence they purport to be is simply bogus. Upon close inspection, it rapidly dissolves.

i) From one work to another and often, Marx speaks of a modification or development of human needs and of the emergence of new needs in the course of history.[92] Correspondingly, he speaks also of a transformation of the nature of man. To give just one example of this from *Capital*: man, he says, 'acts upon external nature and changes it, and in this way he simultaneously changes his own nature'.[93] Assertions of this type are sometimes invoked in support of the disputed claim. It is an elementary logical point, however, that to declare of anything that it changes does not commit one to the view that *everything* about it changes or that it has *no* enduring features. Forecasts of a change in the weather would otherwise be received with much greater anxiety than they generally are. More appositely here, to read the above statement from *Capital* as denying all permanent and general characteristics of a human nature is as justified and sensible as taking it equally for a denial of any constant elements in 'external nature'; that is, not at all so. The latter inference is in fact rather rare though not altogether unknown, for one occasionally encounters the notion that, according to Marx, nature itself is man's creation, a product of history and so forth – a notion whose 'rational kernel' is that Marx does indeed see the natural world as mightily transformed by human activity, but which in such unqualified form reveals nevertheless the flagrant idealism of this whole line of thought. Of course, as the human species is itself a product of evolution, to refer to a constant human make-up, permanent characteristics and so on, is not to talk in absolute terms. But *relatively*, within the temporal range of Marx's historical theory – just a few thousand years and the merest fraction of the evolutionary process – the idea of permanent and general attributes of man is certainly valid. In any case, his many statements about human variation through history are logically compatible with it and therefore no evidence whatever for the contention that he rejected it.

ii) In many passages in *The German Ideology*, Marx criticizes Hegelian and Young Hegelian thought for a speculative and teleological treatment of history and likewise of man. He writes, for example: 'Once . . . the conclusion has been reached that history is always under the sway of ideas, it is very easy to abstract from these various ideas "the Idea", the thought, etc., as the dominant force in history, and thus to consider all these separate ideas and concepts as "forms of self-determination" of the Concept developing in history. It follows then naturally, too, that all the relations of men can be derived from the concept of man, man as conceived, the essence of man, Man. This has been done by speculative philosophy.'[94] Marx, in other words, dismisses the idea that history is the work of some single transcendental subject, be it 'the world spirit', 'self-consciousness' or even 'man'; the act of a 'metaphysical spectre', 'a single individual, which accomplishes the mystery of generating itself'.[95] He dismisses simultaneously the assumption of an original historical destiny or plan, wherein 'man', for instance, is 'the ultimate purpose of world history'; if 'later history is made the goal of earlier history', he says, the real process is 'speculatively distorted'.[96] Now, to the extent that they are applicable to aspects of his own early work,[97] these strictures may be taken as being self-critical as well as other-directed, part of Marx's famous 'settling of accounts',[98] and thus evidence of a certain intellectual break. Once again, however, there is an elementary logical point to be made here. To dismiss *speculative* notions of man is not to dismiss the idea as such of a general human nature or, in particular, a *materialist* concept of it, one based on objective investigation, open to procedures of scientific correction and research. To interpret these passages from *The German Ideology* as disputing the very idea of human nature is therefore merely arbitrary, an unwarranted extension of Marx's own argument.

iii) It is by an equally unwarranted extension of another,

very familiar argument of his that it too is sometimes so interpreted. According to Marx, a standard mechanism in the ideological legitimation of existing social arrangements consists of representing as universal what are in fact historically specific features of them. The institutions of, or traits fostered by, one sort of social order are generalized so as to appear necessary, permanent, indeed *natural*; turned, in the words of the *Communist Manifesto*, 'into eternal laws of nature and of reason'.[99] We have already come across one instance of this recurrent Marxian theme in the earlier-quoted comment upon Bentham to the effect that he naively assumes the modern petty bourgeois to be typical of all humanity.[100] Marx takes Proudhon to task, similarly, for viewing competition as 'a necessity of the *human soul*'.[101] And he argues that it is the appearances of a 'society of free competition' that are universalized, in Smith, Ricardo and the social contract thinkers of the eighteenth century, to produce the isolated and independent individual which is their theoretical point of departure, the individual, as he puts it, 'appropriate to their notion of human nature'.[102] In such arguments as these, Marx is challenging what he considers to be a *false* generalization of attributes which are historically formed and culturally specific. He is seeking also to expose, sometimes explicitly, sometimes only implicitly, its *conservative* ideological function. It should be obvious that to challenge a false or a conservative concept of human nature is not to impugn all concepts of it. To question whether certain, named characteristics are permanent and natural ones is neither to say nor to imply that there are not permanent and natural human characteristics.

iv) Marx speaks in *Capital* of individuals as the 'personifications' and 'bearers' (*Träger*) of economic categories or relations.[103] The asceticism of the capitalist, for example, his drive to accumulate wealth for accumulation's sake, is explained in these terms, as a necessity for one so placed: the 'bearer of this movement [of capital – NG]', 'capital personified', 'cog' in a 'social mechanism', capital's 'mere functionary'.[104] Much has been made of this in recent 'structuralist' renderings of Marx's ideas, and it does embody an important if fairly well-rehearsed historical materialist point concerning the societal bases of individual motivation and action. However, it is idle to pretend that for Marx himself it constitutes an all-embracing *system* of explanation, a comprehensive structuralism putatively disposing of the assumption of human nature. The futility and the capriciousness of interpreting it so emerges in short order. In the first place, with the same ease with which he can say that individuals do personify a social relation, Marx can also, when it suits him, say that they do not. He can distinguish and distance people from, as well as identifying them with, their functions. Thus, with the development of capitalism, he asserts, there is a more extravagant consumption amongst its agents: 'with the growth of accumulation and wealth, the capitalist ceases to be merely the incarnation of capital. He begins to feel a human warmth towards his own Adam'.[105] The capitalist now falls short of the 'ideal' of production for the sake of production.[106] Equally, the worker, described by Marx in one breath as '*labour* personified', is said in the very next to find this labour 'just effort and torment'.[107] The whole mode of discourse is for Marx an adaptable and open one, rubbing shoulders with many another idiom. It is not the closed and self-sufficient metaphysic which some like to foist upon him. Furthermore, it is not only persons but also things that he speaks of as bearers of economic categories and relations: use-values as bearers of value and exchange-value; more generally, material conditions as bearers of a specific social nexus.[108] One might just as well interpret him to mean by this that the material objects and conditions in question lack intrinsic natural properties or can be exhaustively explained by the social relationships which they 'bear'.

v) Closely related to iv), and therefore worth little comment additional to it, are Marx's polemics against those who abstract from differences of class in appealing to a common humanity: like Karl Heinzen, for instance, for whom, he says, 'all classes melt away before the solemn concept of "humanity" . . . Herr Heinzen believes that *whole classes* which are based on *economic* conditions independent of their own will and are forced into the most virulent contradiction by these conditions, can by means of the quality of "humanity", which attaches to all men, shed their real relationships. . .'[109] The scare-quotes around 'humanity' here obviously express a certain sarcasm; as elsewhere, Marx derides a usage of such concepts that belittles or overlooks the interests and constraints of class.[110] And this is, once again, a matter quite central to historical materialism. But, as evidence, it is no better than the language of 'bearers'. To insist upon the importance of class scarcely commits one to denying that individuals share a common human nature. It does not entail that their class is exhaustive of what they are.

All this other evidence, in sum, has no value. It is spurious. In its status as evidence, the most interesting thing about it is that anyone should have considered it to be that. That they have, and in the face of so much from Marx's work proving he did not reject the idea of a human nature, suggests that the notion that he did is probably nourished also by reasons extraneous to direct textual proof. In so far as Marxists themselves have been responsible for propagating it, at work, I think, has been the familiar tendency to want and claim the Old Man's blessing for one's own conception of things. For, with many Marxists, it is indeed their own conviction that there is something mistaken about assuming a universal human nature; that the idea therefore *ought* to be denied. I now go on to argue against reasons generally offered for this view. Hence I stray, finally, beyond the question of interpretation, to urge that not only did Marx not reject the idea of human nature but he was also *right* not to do so. It should go without saying, however, that even if good reasons can be adduced against the concept of human nature, this will not show that Marx himself dispensed with it, only that it is regrettable if he did not. So if some or all of the following argument fails, it has no bearing whatever on the exegetical case which it has been the main purpose of this essay to make. The principal reasons generally given against the idea of a human nature seem to be these.

vi) It is a reactionary one, used against socialism and any project of radical change; put forward in suggesting that some deplorable characteristic or other supportive of an existing social institution or pattern is a permanent and ineradicable part of the human make-up. There is no disputing the frequency of this kind of suggestion: in reference to selfishness, greed, love of power, cruelty; to private property, social and sexual inequality, nationalism, violence and war, as well as any number of other things. However, what is crucial in such arguments from human nature is not that there *is* one but that *these* are its attributes. In response we need only show, or give reasons where we cannot show to hope, that they are not. We have no need to deny that there are some constant attributes constitutive of a human nature. It is just not true that this supposition is in itself politically reactionary. Where it concerns basic human needs, whether for adequate nourishment and other physical provision, for love, respect and friendship, or for a freedom and breadth of intellectual and physical self-expression; where it concerns the identification of suffering and oppression associated with their non-fulfilment, and the attempt to change or remove such institutions as may be responsible for frustrating them – this is surely a central part of any socialist politics worth the name: the fight against what is inimical to human happiness. Could it be reactionary in today's world to protest and act against hunger? Or against torture? And could not one – I do not say the only – motivation for doing so be a conception, an elementary conception, of the vital needs of any healthy human being, in virtue of human nature? The claim that this is a reactionary concept betrays, anyway, a very partial view of its place in the history of social theory. The kind of use of it by Marx that I have documented is a case in point. With its critical and progressive edge, it is in broad conformity with the usage of much socialist, anarchist, communitarian and other radical thought.[111]

vii) The concept, it is also said, is an idealist one. But this is a confusion identical with the last and it merits exactly the same sort of answer: just because there are idealist conceptions of human nature, it does not follow that all conceptions of it are idealist. It is true that under the heading of human nature there often reside what one might call projects of deification; attempts precisely to unshackle humanity from nature, to liberate human beings from, or elevate them above, their own biology and indeed the corruption of materiality itself, by recourse to free will, the soul, notions of pure creativity, the spark of divinity within each person, and so on. Yet it cannot be an appropriate materialist response here simply to assert that, on account of man's social and historical formation, there is no human nature. On the contrary, this risks being but a covert form of the very idealism it purports to challenge. By setting up an absolute distinction between society/history and nature, it divorces humanity from the natural world – in particular from *other species*, which for their part are never denied to possess an intrinsic nature – and functions in this respect exactly like the theological conceptions just mentioned. Against these, any genuine materialism must insist rather that human beings, for all that is distinctive about them as a species, and for all of their traits, activities and relationships which can only be explained by specificities of society and history, are nevertheless, like all other species, material and natural beings; 'irredeemably' rooted in a given biological constitution; *absolutely continuous* with the rest of the natural world. Such insistence betokens an alternative view of human nature, not a denial of it.

viii) The charge of idealism, though, can be intended also in another sense. It is laid by Marxists and Marxists align materialism with science. Those who say the concept of human nature is idealist sometimes appear to mean that, *irrespective* of its specific content (thus of whether it is idealist or materialist in the senses discussed under vii)), in the scientific study of history it is an impediment to sound theory and research. It is a philosophical *generality*, fit only to inhabit speculative treatments of man, a substitute for concrete and detailed empirical investigation. Yet again it must be conceded that the argument has a legitimate target. Human nature can certainly function in this way. It stands in often enough for any real effort to gather objective data; provides the easy, the short-cut answer to questions only genuinely answerable in the light of extensive and painstaking factual enquiry. However, if this alone invalidated the concept, what other concept within Marxist theory would be left intact? There is none that cannot be, and has not been, so abused. Class, state, ideology, productive forces, production relations: how often have they been deployed to block off serious thought and research? This is not in itself proof that they have no valid content and application. There is very good reason to view with suspicion any too facile appeal to ideas of human nature: to consider carefully whether the uniformities and innate characteristics they presuppose can be substantiated by research in the biological, psychological and historical sciences, and to be alert also that, in virtue precisely of their generality, they take us just so far and no further; their explanatory role within history is a limited one. Still, this is to say only that what matters is whether the content of some given generalization concerning a human nature is *true*, and what it is alleged to explain, and whether it actually does explain it – issues I come to in their turn below. One cannot take it as a serious proposition about any concept that just on account of its generality, irrespective of its content, it is incompatible with the theory and procedures of a science.

ix) Next let us consider objection prompted by the normative or moral aspect of the question. Like the charge of idealism, under which some would in any case subsume it, such objection comes in different versions. Statements about human nature, it may be argued on the one hand, are really value judgments. As such, they cannot *be* true, since truth (equally, falsehood) is not a property of the value judgment. Expressing as they do the goals or the interests of those who make them, the ideology perhaps of a class and time, lacking even the possibility of objective validity, they are statements useless from a cognitive point of view. The argument is misguided. Hypotheses about human nature can certainly form part of the basis for normative judgment, a point I proceed to immediately after this. Yet they are not in themselves necessarily instances of it. They may of course be extremely contentious but that is not the same thing. So can any matter of fact. The point is not whether people can or do dispute them, for it is notorious that this happens even with truths supported by over-whelming objective evidence: that the Nazis killed mil-lions of Jews, for example. To everyone but the consistent relativist whom, frankly, I discount, the point rather is whether they are open to being settled by empirical evi-dence, in principle at least. Perhaps it is supposed that no statements having reference to a human nature ever are. But that is surely false. It is a plain fact that human beings, in virtue of their intrinsic make-up, need food and water, sleep, shelter against the elements, sexual gratification; or, in case this is regarded by some as too vulgarly physical, not 'human' enough, that they possess also linguistic, reasoning and productive capacities which between them make possible a purposeful transformation of the envi-ronment such as no other earthly species is capable of. Again, there is a general human capacity to make and enjoy music. With respect to some emotions – namely, anger, disgust, fear, happiness, sadness and surprise – there is compelling evidence not just of their universality, but for a thesis of Darwin's that the facial *expressions* of them are similar regardless of culture, being of biological origin.[112]

Claims about human nature *may* disguise a value judg-ment, in the sense of being motivated psychologically by no more than the wish to commend something or other. Even where they are quite controversial, however, they need not, and should not therefore be presumed to, be so inspired. Consider, for instance, Marx's assertion of a human need for breadth and variety of activity. Some would no doubt challenge it as being merely an arbitrary generalization of what he himself happened to think desirable. Yet it does not have to be so. We can construe it as an empirical hypothesis: that in general people will themselves be happier with such breadth and variety than without it, happier than they will constrained to a very narrow range of pursuit; and will, given the choice of the former, in fact choose it. To provide evidence for this is in practice certainly a more complex and difficult enterprise than where needs of bare survival are concerned. And, as is true of many hypotheses which are a premise of socialist and other radical aims – that a genuine socialist democracy, for example, is workable in a large, industrial society – conclusive evidence for it on a society-wide scale could only be gained in future and from social practices and institutions yet to be created.[113] The theoretical test is also part of a long historical battle – which may in the end be lost. Nevertheless, in principle the hypothesis should be susceptible to confirmation or refutation. That, in any case, is how I think Marx himself viewed it. For what it is worth, I think, too, the hypothesis is true and that much could be adduced to support it even now. I do not intend, though, to argue this here since my concern is not to vindicate everything *in* Marx's conception of human nature but only, having shown that he did rely upon one, to defend him for having done so. Those inclined to be sceptical about a human need for the sort of free scope he had in mind might perhaps just ask themselves whether they do not already enjoy much more of it than most people.

x) On the other hand, even if statements about human nature are not themselves necessarily value judgments, the role that they can and do play in contributing to the reasons for these make them an object of distrust for those Marxists who believe that Marxism can have nothing to do with moral judgment beyond seeking to explain it in

the mouths of others. For them the very idea of a normative dimension to Marxism, and the idea in turn of a
human nature for being associated, howsoever, with one –
together these bite the dust. Now there are large and interesting questions about the place of moral concepts within
Marxist thought. For example, did Marx, as some
philosophers affirm and other philosophers deny, con-
demn capitalist society in the light of a conception of justice? And how can one reconcile his criticism, even
ridicule, of the ethical pronouncements of others with his
own censure, manifest and scathing, of the exploitative
and oppressive features of that society? How interpret the
relationship between what one might call the 'sociology'
of ethics implicit in his theory of ideology and such idea of
'the good' as he himself entertained? Did Marx, as I would
hold to be so although it is often gainsaid, accept the distinction between fact and value? Can Marxism accommodate a conception of human rights and, if so, what relation
might it bear to basic and other human needs? These are
important questions and debated to some profit, but they
are not the subject of this essay; they would require
another at least as long.

It is sufficient to my purposes to say that an ethical
position resting upon a conception of human nature is a
perfectly possible one, possible in the sense of being logically unobjectionable, coherent in principle. If one places a
value upon human life and human happiness and there
exist universal needs that must be satisfied respectively to
preserve and to promote these, then this furnishes, the
value and the fact conjointly, a basis for normative judgment: such needs ought to be satisfied *ceteris paribus*.[114]
With regard, as it happens, to the most fundamental needs,
it is the view of some philosophers that this is not just a
possible ethical standpoint but a necessary one; any moral

system logically *must* lay an obligation upon people to try to meet each other's needs of survival. I am not persuaded of that, but it would require once again more discussion than there is space for here to spell out why, and more discussion also than is to the point. For whether this ethical position is indeed necessary or is only possible, it is in any case possible, since it has to be possible to be necessary in the relevant sense. Either way, what I have documented as clearly present in Marx's work, labelling it the normative function or usage of his idea of human nature, can be defended as a possible, a logically coherent, viewpoint.

What of the argument that Marxism has no room for any such normative dimension? Leave aside as germane to the previous rather than this section of the present essay that, in so far as the argument is meant to apply to the doctrines actually propagated by Karl Marx, it is a piece of the most pure obscurantism, and the cleverest procedures of 'reading' will not suffice to hide this. Whatever answers are proferred to the question of the place of moral concepts in Marx's thought, they must, to carry any weight at all, be consistent with the obvious presence in his writings of a conception of the human good – in that broad sense at least, with the presence of a moral doctrine. Leaving that, as I say, aside, those Marxists who argue for a Marxism lacking the latter feature may be asked to state what reasons they have and can give others for thinking social-ism to be a desirable objective and worth striving for, and exploitation and its correlates matters for condemnation; for they invariably do think this despite every disclaimer. If they can give reasons why they do, then their standpoint is by contrast with the one defended here simply incoher-ent, at once possessing and disowning an evaluative dimension. If they have no reasons, they should cease to speak as if they thought in this way. At any rate, a thought without reasons does not especially recommend itself as against one with them. And if the case is indeed that here are Marxists who really do not think socialism a worthwhile objective or exploitation wrong, who refrain from normative judgment and are wont to speak accordingly – though I should like and have yet to encounter, in person or print, just one true exemplar of the phenomenon – then there is consistency in that; but what else apart from consistency might be supposed to commend such an outlook to others? Particularly within a tradition of thought engaged from its very inception in a movement and a struggle for practical goals as well as in empirical theory and research. One can as a logical possibility consistently disown all moral evaluation of social realities, but then one is tied by nothing at all to the aim of a better human existence, free of starvation, toil, domination, warfare and so on. This may, perhaps, still leave a Marxism of sorts. It is a mere stipulation that Marxism as such has to be of that character.

xi) I turn now to a sort of reasoning met with often in direct discussion and in the nature of a tactical retreat, so to speak. Its proponent begins by disputing the existence of a human nature, then when confronted with the undeniable fact of some general human needs, powers or other uniformities, says something along the following lines: 'Oh well . . . all this is, of course, obvious, so obvious as to be scarcely worth mentioning; for present purposes (discussion of Marx or Marxism, society, politics, history, etc.) it is of little or no importance.' By the combination of these charges – extreme obviousness on the one hand and extreme unimportance on the other – the hope is to consign to the margins of serious consideration a concept which can no longer be straightforwardly denied. I separate the two issues and take them in turn.

As to obviousness, three brief comments will suffice. First, in so far as the truth of some generalizations regarding shared human characteristics *is* obvious, this is an argument in favour of the idea of a human nature and not against it. Second, there can be a point in stating the obvious in certain contexts. One of these arises when falsehoods and absurdities are being maintained – such as are commonly attributed to Marx in this very connection. I might say here in passing that I am all too well aware of the obviousness of much of what I have been obliged to argue in this essay. It is due precisely to the absurdity of the view of Marx I have sought to criticize; and justified, perhaps, by the contribution I hope the essay may make to laying that absurdity finally to rest. Thirdly, and as we have already had occasion to note, there are claims about human nature whose truth is *not* obvious, but controversial. People reduced to complaining of how uninteresting are the obviously true ones – though having themselves, in no small number of cases, overlooked them but a moment before – can be encouraged to take an interest in these others.

xii) Worth somewhat more attention is the second issue, concerning the importance to be attached to the existence of universal human characteristics. Some think by belittling it to save the substance of argumentation against a human nature even while conceding that there is one: yes, so it will be said, such universal characteristics are (after all) a fact, but it is a fact of trivial significance. As estimates of this sort require some estimative context, let me suggest a couple of such contexts (relevant to discussion of Marx or Marxism, society, politics, history, etc.) wherein the fact in question can be seen, on the contrary, to be most significant.

A first, immediate and urgent *practical* one, showing

why it is not only true but also important that human beings need food, a healthy living and working environment and so on, can be overlooked only by very secluded and comfortable minds. This context is – that 40,000 children die every day; that of the 122 million born in 1979, 17 million (nearly 14 per cent) will die before they are five; that between 350 and 500 million people are disabled, the major cause of this being poverty: about 100 million have been disabled by malnutrition; that 180 million children are not getting enough food to sustain health and minimal physical activity: protein deficiency, which can lead to mental retardation, affects 100 million under five in developing countries, around 6000 children go blind every year in Tamil Nadu alone because their diets lack vitamin A, and there are in Bangladesh something between 50,000 and 200,000 blind children; that over half the people in the third world have no access to safe water and that water-borne diseases kill some 30,000 people every day and account for about 80 per cent of all illnesses: every year 400 to 500 million are affected by trachoma and six million children die of diarrhoea; that there are 15 million human beings who have been disabled by their work; that in the tin mines of Bolivia a miner's life expectancy is reduced to 35 because of silicosis and tuberculosis; that 375,000 or more people in the third world will this year be poisoned by pesticides. . . And all this is to say nothing of the brutalities directly meted out in many countries by agents of the state: of the beating, the burning, the cutting, the drowning.

It will be urged that these realities are conspicuously *historical* and *political* ones. Of course they are, but they have an irreducible 'human-natural' component: of general and basic human needs, in this case unsatisfied, disregarded, thwarted, sometimes savagely repressed. The moral, if not the sheer numerical, enormity of them has something to do with that. And although they are realities contemporary with ourselves rather than with Marx, they are of a kind with ones he manifestly regarded, and publicized, as 'significant'. In what present socialist political perspective could they be regarded otherwise?

There is also an apposite *theoretical* context and it is this that they themselves are most likely to have in mind who disparage the importance of the idea of a human nature. Even if it does denote something real, they will say, still it has no role within Marxist theory; it does not and cannot explain anything. Thus one writer, sympathetically explicating the materialist conception of history according to Althusser, speaks of 'rejection of any notion of human nature in general, at least of any such notion which involve(s) a claim to an explanatory role in the science of history'.[115] The 'at least' clause somewhat softens the point being made here and may be read as an abbreviated version of the sort of common retreat I have been talking about. It does not soften it enough, however, to render it defensible. In relation to the theory of history put forth by Marx himself, we have seen already that this point is in fact false. A concept of human nature, encompassing at once the common needs and the general and distinctive capacities of humankind, plays an important, a quite fundamental, explanatory role there in accounting for those specifically human social relationships that are production relations and for that specifically human type of process of change that is history.[116] We can now generalize what is implicit in this and show that, independently of the accurate interpretation of Marx, those who wish to deny human nature a significant explanatory role within historical materialism are guilty of a false contrast and a logical incoherence. For what they invariably maintain is that such a role falls *rather* to 'the ensemble of social relations' or something similar: society, the social formation or social whole, the mode, or the relations, of production. Try, then, simply to define what these concepts mean – *ab initio*; to elaborate their content without assuming any prior knowledge of it. It will prove necessary, in doing so, to say at some point both that they have to do with relations involving human beings and what kind of beings these are. This is not a merely verbal point (whatever that might be) but one of substance; because there are features of the relations in question that are due precisely to the *nature of the entities they relate*, that is to say, to the general make-up of human beings, to human nature. The latter is therefore a constitutive element in any concept of the ensemble of social relations, a view of it, either explicit or implicit, absolutely necessary to any social theory, and discounting its theoretical role while simultaneously talking, under whatever name, about *human* society, a logical absurdity. The supposed replacement of the idea of human nature by the central concepts of historical materialism, that theoretical incompatibility alleged here by 'theoretical anti-humanism', is merely bombast.

It is true, certainly, that one can overstate how much it is possible to explain by reference to human nature, and Marxists are good at noticing the danger, which is just as well since all manner of historically parochial phenomena, from capitalist competition to nationalism and the State, are sometimes so explained. It is also true, however, that one can understate it and, in the context of historical materialism, the temptation to do so has become endemic. At the cost of repeating a point, therefore, but so as to counteract as emphatically as possible the style of argument to the contrary so often met with, it bears saying again: *historical materialism itself, this whole distinctive approach to society that originates with Marx, rests squarely upon the idea of a human nature.* It highlights that specific nexus of universal needs and capacities which explains the human production process and man's organized transformation of the material environment; which process and transformation it treats in turn as the basis both of the social order and of historical change.[117] So, it is not even true, in other words, although frequently supposed, that being for its part general and unchanging, human nature cannot itself enter into the explanation of change.[118] On the contrary, if human beings have a history which gives rise to the most fabulous variety of social shapes and forms, it is because of the kind of beings they, all of them, are; human nature, to allude once more to my initial distinction, plays a part in explaining the historical specificities of the nature of man. We can point to many other things obviously also presupposed by the theory: the common capacity, wide variation of form again notwithstanding, for the complex communication involved in human language and for cultural and artistic symbolism more generally; the formulation and observance of *norms* or rules. These are general human characteristics. Or, moving further away from the theory's central preoccupations – though this matter surely bears a close relation to that of art and culture – we can point to the existence in all societies and from early infancy of games and other forms of play. If the diversity of these, the particularities of one or another, will call for a discriminating historical and social explanation, the need for and enjoyment of play itself is just a feature of humanity as such, rooted in its biological nature. Such facts as these are so fundamental that one is entitled much of the time to take them for granted. But if, doing so, one then *forgets* them and says that there are no such facts, is no human nature and so forth, one falls into a kind of nonsense.[119]

This puts us in a position to dispose in short order of two other common arguments, mere variants, in effect, of that challenging the importance of truths about human nature. Before proceeding to them, however, we may notice one more thing here, an area in which practical and theoretical aspects, considered above one beside the other, can be seen clearly to overlap.

Marxists and socialists dismissive of the assumption of an intrinsic human nature are generally committed to the project, and believe in or at least are not dissuaded of the possibility, of a radically different social order, however variously they may conceive this. They must believe, consequently, or must allow, that people in their generality can, or might, develop the qualities that will sustain such a social order, whatever these qualities may be thought to be: civic intelligence, interest, responsibility; mutual sympathy or respect, a deep feeling of human equality, the ability to use and enjoy a very extensive individual freedom; and so on (for present purposes, the precise shape of this list does not especially matter; each person may construct her own). The whole weight is placed, with this sort of belief and by this sort of Marxist and socialist, upon the anticipated effect of new social relations and practices. Yet, although much weight properly belongs there, by itself this will not quite do. If new relations and practices are thought able to have the effect in question, human beings must be assumed *capable*, if only in the 'right' circumstances, of developing the necessary qualities. These must be capacities potentially available to members of the human species. Just as no fish could have been Mozart, no species could achieve socialism if the generality of its members were inherently incapable in all conditions of the virtues appropriate to socialism. Of course, this is exactly how many of the latter's opponents view things: that irrespective of historical circumstances, the generality of humankind will be stupid or ignorant rather than intelligent, apathetic instead of interested, in awe of leaders and not capable of genuine responsibility; and too selfish, greedy and competitive to sustain any wide sense of human solidarity or community; afraid of too much freedom and unable to use it. A string of conservative, elitist and anti-democratic thinkers could here be cited. The point, though, is this. It is quite specious to contend that those only who thus deny, but not also those who affirm, the possibility of socialism, rely upon a conception of human nature. For the affirmation just presupposes the sort of human capacities that the denial disputes. Hence, the standard practical commitment within Marxist and socialist belief rests, whether explicitly or implicitly, upon the theoretical hypothesis of a human nature – at least if it is to have a coherent theoretical basis.

xiii) Historical materialism, it is sometimes argued, does not *begin from* the idea of a human nature inherent in individuals but rather from their social relations; or again, it takes the latter instead of the former as theoretically *basic*.[120] This argument has been all but dealt with already under xii). To what was said there we need only add that if those concepts themselves identified as the theory's point of departure or basis cannot even be explicated without reference to a concept of human nature, then it has an equal claim with them to being a constituent of that point of departure or basis. The view now and again expressed that to admit as much is tantamount to methodological individualism is unfounded. That an intrinsic human make-up enters into the explanation of man's basic social relations entails neither that it explains them and their variation completely, nor that social reality can be reduced without residue to the actions and purposes of individuals, nor that social structures and processes do not for their part have an enormous weight in the explanation of the overall character of these individuals. One is not bound to think within the false polarities some would impose here.

xiv) 'A structure determines its elements'. This formula too, the formula of so-called structural causality, is already more or less taken care of by the discussion at xii). It will have a bearing on argument against a human nature only if 'determines' is given the strong sense earlier defined, according to which one thing determines another when the second depends completely upon the first. If, in that case, it is proposed as an empirical claim that the structure *of social relations* determines its elements, then the claim is false since the character of these particular elements, so far from depending completely upon this structure, explains something of *its* character. And if, on the other hand, the formula is meant to be definitive of what a structure is, then the structure of social relations is not a structure in the stipulated sense, and that for exactly the same reason.

xv) There is, finally, one other argument, which serves those who have recourse to it as a kind of licence for inconsistency. By this I do not mean, of course, that they use it with the deliberate intention of being inconsistent. I mean only that it enables them to accommodate their inconsistency with a degree of intellectual comfort. The denial of a human nature is, I have said, an absurdity. Many manage to get by with this absurdity because, in making the denial, they fail to 'notice', i.e., they give no theoretical weight or prominence to, realities with which one must assume them to be acquainted on some level or other. This failure is not universal however. There are some who, in impugning the idea of a human nature, go out of their way nonetheless to insist upon the relevance and importance of the fact that the social relations are precisely relations between human beings; to stress that human beings are subject to common natural or biological as well as to social determinants, and so on.[121] The trouble with such otherwise unobjectionable declarations is that anything offered in elaboration of them, anything by way of filling out their content, will itself provide a concept of human nature, no more and no less. This is where the argument licensing inconsistency comes in; and it goes as follows: although there are, to be sure, certain general, biologically based characteristics of humankind, they do not exist as a distinct or separate reality; they cannot be isolated *ontologically* from the social determinants with which they are indissolubly compounded. What we mean by human nature, in other words, is never found in pure form. It is always 'socially mediated'.[122] By this sort of argument, one can hope to make use of both sides of a contradiction, relying now on the one by calling in question any talk of a human nature, and now on the other by talking of what is natural to human beings.[123]

We should inspect more closely the reasoning that seeks to legitimate this obfuscation. It states an important truth. For all that it does so, however, this truth is frequently misused. More significantly, it is irrelevant to the argument for and against the existence or reality of a human nature. I enlarge on these two contentions and conclude.

A favourite text in this regard is the following sentence from Marx's 1857 *Introduction*: 'Hunger is hunger, but the hunger gratified by cooked meat eaten with a knife and fork is a different hunger from that which bolts down raw meat with the aid of hand, nail and tooth'.[124] In most circumstances it would be unnecessary to remark that Marx makes reference here not only to a difference, even if that is where his emphasis obviously lies, but also to an identity – 'Hunger is hunger . . .' He speaks of a difference, but between two ways of satisfying a common human need. In the present context, it *is* necessary to remark upon this because of the manner in which the point of his sentence, together with the more general one he is arguing in this place – namely, that production not only meets, it also shapes, the needs of consumption – is often exaggerated; used even to advocate a social or a structural *as opposed to* an anthropological theory of needs. The opposition is unacceptable. Notwithstanding the rich variety which processes of socialization impose upon the patterns of human need, this influence obviously has its limits, natural limits governed by the sort of creatures we are. Thus although, for example, we would have no need for cooking oil if we did not have the use of fire or electricity, not just anything will adequately meet this need, as has been most gruesomely demonstrated in Spain of late by the sale of a poisonous substance in the guise of cooking oil. More generally, food may be taken, offered, received, thought of, in countless ways. Indeed, what some regard as food, others will not. But, again, not just anything can be food. And even narrowing our focus down to what can, not all of it is equally nourishing or conducive to health (another fact, incidentally, both of explanatory significance and of practical importance for socialists).

Hunger is hunger, and people die of it; or have to live with it or with irremediable disabilities that are due to it. When someone dies of or is disabled by it, *whatever* the social causes of this may be, there are also proximate causes that are not culturally specific: the body's lack of proteins, vitamins, nourishment. Furthermore, it is generally true, irrespective of socialization and despite cases of strong cultural taboo, that the hungrier you get the less it will matter what there is to eat, only provided there is something. To inflate the difference registered in Marx's sentence until it altogether overshadows the identity, to obliterate the existence of a common human nature here, of the common need for food and of the common experience of starvation which follows when it is not met, is to misuse the truth he states. Must we then say that two children crying in the night do not share the emotion of fear because their time or place and their language are different (and fear too can be a factor within historical explanation)? Or that, because they express whatever they do express in a different language, it is not a common human capacity they make use of in doing so? Or, again, that within the wide variety of sexual desire and sexual joy there is no common experience associated with, for example, orgasm? How culturally specific are the ways of bleeding, sleeping, walking, running, grasping a tool in the hand – or is the feeling of acute physical pain? The end point of the whole line of reasoning is a cultural relativism gone quite beserk.

It is, however, the second of my two contentions that is the more crucial here. For, of course, one need not exaggerate the truth of Marx's observation until it turns into a falsehood. One can use it with due sense of proportion; use it indeed to salutary effect in laying down some basic propositions of historical materialism. Still, even so, it is not relevant to the question in dispute. That the general, natural characteristics of human beings are not found in a pure state, so to speak, but only socially mediated; that they do not form a *separate* reality, ontologically distinct from qualities that are culturally induced – this is not germane to the validity of the concept of human nature. It is no argument against the reality or existence of what the latter denotes. Consider what is entailed by the view that it is a compelling argument. We should have always to reject a concept, as we are advised in the present case to reject that of a human nature, when what it was the concept of could not be isolated ontologically and found standing 'on its own'. A clear analytical distinction would be insufficient; existential separateness would always be required as well. We should have then, in the first place, to reject (as the proponents of this view do not and nor, for obvious reasons, is it logically open to them to) the concept of the relations of production. These do not exist in ontological isolation, separate from other social realities, legal, political, ideological, and so on. Existentially, they are themselves most thoroughly interrelated with such other realities. It scarcely makes sense to talk of relations of production as an isolated reality or existing on their own. This is, therefore, an abstraction. But it is a valid one and denotes a definite reality. If that were to be denied, how could one meaningfully claim the relations of production have real effects? It is exactly the same with the idea of a human nature. It is an abstraction but a valid one, denoting some common, natural characteristics of humankind. These may not be a *separate* reality, ontologically distinct and what have you, but *they are a reality*. One cannot sensibly deny this and speak simultaneously of natural or biological 'determinants' with real effects.

We can go further than we have. After the relations of production, we can query whether the State is ontologically separate, and reject any concept of it because it is not. The same with any notion of ideology and of class struggle and of the rate of profit and of national identity, etc. We will be left with no concepts or distinctions in face, simply, of 'the totality'. The argument, in short, is a confusion; exploiting the intimate and fundamental interconnection of everything, if I may so put it, in order to obscure a perfectly clear and viable conceptual distinction. That it is a confusion is indicated by the way in which it homes in arbitrarily on just one of Marx's concepts when, for all that the argument says, it could lay the whole lot of them equally low. That is the sure sign too of a groundless prejudice.

The sixth thesis does not show Marx rejected the idea of a human nature. Marx did not reject the idea of a human nature. He was right not to do so.

Notes

1. I refer to G. A. Cohen, *Karl Marx's Theory of History: A Defence*, Oxford 1978, pp. 150–152; Michael Evans, *Karl Marx*, London 1975, p. 53; and Helmut Fleischer, *Marxism and History*, London 1973, pp. 25–26, 46. See also John McMurtry, *The Structure of Marx's World-View*, Princeton 1978, pp. 19–37; Bertell Ollman, *Alienation: Marx's Conception of Man in Capitalist Society*, Cambridge 1971, p. 76; and Gajo Petrovic, *Marx in the Mid-Twentieth Century*, New York 1967, pp. 73–74.

2. See below, i) of Section IV.

3. All italics are in the original unless otherwise stated. Karl Marx and Frederick Engels, *Collected Works* (referred to henceforth as CW), London 1975ff, Vol. 5, pp. 4–5. The German, in the Marx-Engels *Werke*, Berlin 1956 ff, Vol. 3, pp. 6–7, is:

'Feuerbach löst das religiöse Wesen in das *menschliche* Wesen auf. Aber das menschliche Wesen ist kein dem einzelnen Individuum inwohnendes Abstraktum. In seiner Wirklichkeit ist es das ensemble der gesellschaftlichen Verhältnisse.

'Feuerbach, der auf die Kritik dieses wirklichen Wesens nicht eingeht, ist daher gezwungen:

'1. von dem geschichtlichen Verlauf zu abstrahieren und das religiöse Gemüt für sich zu fixieren, und ein abstrakt – *isoliert* – menschliches Individuum vorauszusetzen.

'2. Das Wesen kann daher nur als "Gattung", als innere, stumme, die vielen Individuen *natürlich* verbindende Allgemeinheit gefasst werden.

'Feuerbach sieht daher nicht, dass das "religiöse Gemüt"

selbst ein gesellschaftliches Produkt ist und dass das abstrakte Individuum, das er analysiert, einer bestimmten Gesellschaftsform angehört.'

4. See for example CW, Vol. 3, pp. 204, 217.

5. Letter to Arnold Ruge, 13 March 1843, CW, Vol. 1, p. 400. The *Theses* were probably written in April 1845.

6. The point can be made equally well if the German phrase 'ist kein . . . Abstraktum' is rendered 'is not an abstraction. . .' (as it is in T. B. Bottomore and Maximilien Rubel (eds.), *Karl Marx: Selected Writings in Sociology and Social Philosophy*, Harmondsworth 1963, p. 83). I do not necessarily deny that the University of Manchester is a collection of buildings, if I say 'The University of Manchester is not a collection of buildings; it is a living intellectual community'.

7. See Cohen, *Karl Marx's Theory of History*, pp. 35–37.

8. See CW, Vol. 5, p. 585 n. 1, and Engels's Foreword to *Ludwig Feuerbach and the End of Classical German Philosophy* in Karl Marx and Frederick Engels, *Selected Works*, Moscow 1969–70, Vol. 3, p. 336.

9. *The Civil War in France* in *Selected Works*, Vol. 2, p. 235.

10. Karl Marx, *A Contribution to the Critique of Political Economy*, London 1971, pp. 20–21.

11. Tom Bottomore, 'Is There a Totalitarian View of Human Nature?', *Social Research*, Vol. 40 No. 3, Autumn 1973 ('Human Nature: A Reevaluation'), p. 435; Robert D. Cumming, 'Is Man Still Man?', Ibid., p. 482; Eugene Kamenka, *The Ethical Foundations of Marxism*, London 1972, p. 146; Louis Althusser, *For Marx*, London 1969, pp. 227–228; Wal Suchting, 'Marx's *Theses on Feuerbach*: Notes Towards a Commentary' in John Mepham and David-Hillel Ruben (eds.), *Issues in Marxist Philosophy*, Vol. 2, Brighton 1979, p. 19; Vernon Venable, *Human Nature: The Marxian View*, Gloucester, Mass. 1975, pp. 20, 4, 22.

12. Robert Tucker, *Philosophy and Myth in Karl Marx*, Cambridge 1961, pp. 165–166; Kate Soper, 'Marxism, Materialism and Biology' in Mepham and Ruben, *Issues in Marxist Philosophy*, Vol. 2, pp. 75, 99; Colin Sumner, *Reading Ideologies*, London 1979, p. 48; Suchting, 'Marx's *Theses on Feuerbach*: Notes Towards a Commentary', p. 19; Venable, *Human Nature: The*

Marxian View, p. 20; Sidney Hook, *From Hegel to Marx*, Ann Arbor 1962, pp. 297–298.

13. *For Marx*, pp. 227–228. The argument is echoed in *Reading Capital*: speaking of the assumptions underlying, successively, 'classical political economy', 'liberal bourgeois optimism' and 'the moral protests of Ricardo's socialist commentators', Althusser says, 'the content of the anthropology changes but the anthropology survived'; on the other hand, 'anthropology's theoretical pretensions have been shattered by Marx's analysis'. Louis Althusser and Etienne Balibar, *Reading Capital*, London 1970, pp. 163, 166.

14. *For Marx*, p. 227.

15. Ibid. p. 229.

16. *Reading Capital*, pp. 180, 253, 267, 268.

17. Andrew Collier, 'Truth and Practice', *Radical Philosophy*, No. 5, Summer 1973, p. 16.

18. Istvan Meszaros, *Marx's Theory of Alienation*, London 1970, pp. 13–14, 148, 170. For the other side of the story see pp. 79, 118, 149, 157, 162, 166, etc.

19. *For Marx*, p. 243; Suchting, 'Marx's *Theses on Feuerbach*: Notes Towards a Commentary', p. 19; Soper, 'Marxism, Materialism and Biology', p. 75. Althusser's metaphor for the enigmatic character of the *Theses* is used as epigraph to this essay: see *For Marx*, p. 36.

20. Engels, Foreword to *Ludwig Feuerbach and the End of Classical German Philosophy, Selected Works*, Vol. 3, p. 336.

21. CW, Vol. 5, p. 55.

22. CW, Vol. 4, p. 141.

23. CW, Vol. 5, p. 254.

24. CW, Vol. 4, p. 36.

25. CW, Vol. 5, p. 289.

26. See David McLellan, *Karl Marx: His Life and Thought*, London 1973, p. 151.

27. CW, Vol. 5, pp. 31–32.

28. The German is 'fällt zusammen mit'.

29. CW, Vol. 5, p. 31.

30. Ibid.

31. CW, Vol. 5, pp. 43–44.

32. CW, Vol. 5, p. 82; 'the reality of their conditioned nature' translates 'ihrer wirklichen Bedingtheit'.

33. CW, Vol. 5, p. 437; 'needs' is italicized in the original – the remaining emphasis is mine.

34. CW, Vol. 5, pp. 44, 57.

35. CW, Vol. 5, pp. 41–42.

36. See n. 13 above.

37. CW, Vol. 5, p. 43.

38. CW, Vol. 5, p. 256. This is from a passage crossed out in the manuscript; but it is legitimate to draw on it in so far as it only confirms what can be established independently.

39. CW, Vol. 5, p. 38.

40. CW, Vol. 5, p. 41.

41. Ibid.

42. CW, Vol. 5, pp. 255, 439, 78.

43. CW, Vol. 5, pp. 255, 256.

44. CW, Vol. 5, pp. 64, 47.

45. CW, Vol. 5, pp. 74, 87, 79.

46. CW, Vol. 5, p. 79.

47. CW, Vol. 5, pp. 87, 425.

48. CW, Vol. 5, pp. 432, 394.

49. CW, Vol. 5, pp. 431–432.

50. CW, Vol. 3, p. 175.

51. CW, Vol. 3, p. 182.

52. CW, Vol. 3, p. 217.

53. CW, Vol. 3, p. 299.

54. Karl Marx, *Capital*, Vol. I (Penguin edition), Harmondsworth 1976, pp. 758–759.

55. Karl Marx, *Capital*, Vol. III, Moscow 1962, p. 800.

56. Karl Marx, *Grundrisse*, Harmondsworth 1973, p. 488.

57. Karl Marx, *Theories of Surplus Value*, Moscow 1968–72, Vol. II, pp. 117–118.

58. *Capital* I, pp. 647, 664, 526–527; *Capital* III, p. 837.

59. *Grundrisse*, p. 84; and cf. *Capital* I, p. 144 n.

60. *Capital* I, pp. 443–444.

61. *Capital* I, p. 447.

62. *Capital* I, pp. 135, 270.

63. *Capital* I, p. 283.

64. *Capital* I, p. 133.

65. *Capital* I, p. 290; and cf. 'Results of the Immediate Process of Production', printed as an Appendix to this volume, p. 998.

66. *Capital* I, pp. 283–4, 287, 290; cf. here, incidentally, CW, Vol. 1, pp. 166–167.

67. *Capital* I, p. 286.

68. 'Results of the Immediate Process of Production', pp. 1021–1022.

69. *Grundrisse*, p. 245.

70. *Capital* I, pp. 275, 277, 341; cf. *Capital* III, p. 837.

71. Except for the last item, this list is constructed from: *Capital* I, pp. 275, 341, 375–376, 621; *Capital* III, pp. 826, 854. For the last item, see: *Capital* I, pp. 552–553, 586, 591; *Capital* III, p. 86.

72. *Capital* I, pp. 345, 381, 599.

73. *Capital* I, pp. 553, 591, 599; *Capital* III, p. 86.

74. *Capital* I, pp. 592, 356, 375–376.

75. *Capital* III, p. 252; *Capital* I, pp. 813, 799, 381.

76. *Capital* I, p. 376.

77. *Capital* I, pp. 517, 591, 618, 638; *Capital* III, p. 793.

78. *Capital* III, p. 86.

79. *Capital* I, pp. 618, 638.

80. 'Results of the Immediate Process of Production', p. 1037.

81. *Capital* I, pp. 772, 375, 460; *Theories of Surplus Value* III, p. 256.

82. *Capital* I, p. 138; *Grundrisse*, p. 611.

83. CW, Vol. 6, p. 506; *Selected Works*, Vol. 3, p. 19.

84. *Grundrisse*, pp. 706, 711; *Capital* I, p. 667. And cf. *Grundrisse*, pp. 158, 708; *Capital* I, p. 618; *Capital* III, p. 854.

85. *Theories of Surplus Value* III, p. 257; *Capital* III, p. 800.

86. *Capital* I, pp. 739, 614; and cf. p. 638.

87. *Grundrisse*, p. 611; *Capital* I, p. 799; 'Results of the Immediate Process of Production', p. 989; *Theories of Surplus Value* III, p. 257.

88. *Capital* I, pp. 547, 614.

89. *Capital* I, pp. 469, 474, 481, 484, 614, 615.

90. *Capital* I, pp. 638, 548.

91. *Capital* I, pp. 523, 547, 614, 799.

92. See CW, Vol. 5, p. 42 and Vol. 6, p. 117; *Grundrisse*, pp.

408–410; *Capital* I, pp. 275, 341, 647, 649, 701; *Capital* III, pp. 799–800, 837.

93. *Capital* I, p. 283; and cf. *The Poverty of Philosophy*: 'history is nothing but a continuous transformation of human nature'. CW, Vol. 6, p. 192.

94. CW, Vol. 5, p. 61.

95. CW, Vol. 5, pp. 51–52, 88–89.

96. CW, Vol. 5, pp. 81, 486, 50; and cf. pp. 57, 293, 305.

97. See, for example, CW, Vol. 3, pp. 304–306, 332–333.

98. *Contribution to the Critique of Political Economy*, p. 22.

99. CW, Vol. 6, p. 501.

100. See the text to n. 54 above.

101. CW, Vol. 6, p. 192.

102. *Grundrisse*, p. 83.

103. *Capital* I, pp. 92, 179; *Capital* III, pp. 804, 857–858.

104. *Capital* I, pp. 254, 739; *Theories of Surplus Value* I, p. 282.

105. *Capital* I, p. 740.

106. *Theories of Surplus Value* I, p. 282.

107. 'Results of the Immediate Process of Production', p. 989.

108. *Capital* I, pp. 126, 138, 293; *Capital* III, pp. 798, 806.

109. CW, Vol. 6, p. 330.

110. Cf. CW, Vol. 6, p. 511.

111. Some of what Marx says in passing about women, however, suggests assumptions that would need to be excluded from this evaluation.

112. It may be of interest to note, incidentally, that the list of general human needs proposed by one recent writer in speaking for his part of an 'innate human nature' is pretty well, though not exactly, identical with that construable from *The German Ideology*. See Barrington Moore, *Injustice. The Social Bases of Obedience and Revolt*, London 1978, p. 6, and the text preceding n. 42 above.

113. See the pertinent remarks at the beginning of David Beetham's 'Beyond Liberal Democracy'. *The Socialist Register*, 1981.

114. *'Ceteris paribus'* in case the goods secured thereby are outweighed by the bads – and judged, this, according either to the same values or to others that might be held side by side with

them. Suppose, as I am sure to be false, there was a universal instinct of physical cruelty, the restraint or even sublimation of which left the individual to whom these applied less contented or fulfilled than would its unrestrained expression. That it was, to this extent, a need in every person would not *ipso facto* render it worthy of being met. Satisfaction of it could be opposed out of considerations of *overall* welfare, or of individual rights, or in the light of other values.

115. Alex Callinicos, *Althusser's Marxism*, London 1976, p. 69.

116. See the text to notes 29–38 above.

117. Cf. Fleischer, *Marxism and History*, p. 49; and Andrew Collier, 'Materialism and Explanation in the Human Sciences' in Mepham and Ruben, *Issues in Marxist Philosophy*, Vol. 2, pp. 44–45.

118. On this, see Cohen's remarks: *Karl Marx's Theory of History*, p. 152.

119. See, in this connection, Sebastiano Timpanaro's nice metaphor concerning the first-floor tenant's contempt for the tenant on the floor below. *On Materialism*, London 1975, pp. 44–45.

120. See the statements of Suchting at notes 11 and 12 above – and compare these with Marx's at n. 29.

121. John Mepham, 'Who Makes History?', *Radical Philosophy* 6, Winter 1973; Kate Soper, 'Marxism, Materialism and Biology'. And see also Kate Soper, 'On Materialisms', *Radical Philosophy* 15, Autumn 1976, at pp. 15–17, 20.

122. This argument pervades Soper's article – see, for example, 'Marxism, Materialism and Biology', pp. 61–62, 71–72, 77, 92–93– and something similar is suggested by Mepham; see p. 26.

123. Thus Mepham suggests that the idea of a human nature and the theory of the class struggle are 'conceptually incompatible' (p. 25) and can refer accordingly to the 'inadequacy' of the concept of 'men' and even the 'absence of "men" in *Capital*' (pp. 27–28); and says *also* that 'human social relations are only possible because they involve ... *men* and not, say, rocks or dogs'. There may be, it turns out, a valid concept of 'men', only it could not be the same one as inhabits the 'pre-Marxian prob-

lematic' or the 'ideological discourse of everyday life' (pp. 26–27) – which comes down to saying that Marx (for it is a defence of Althusser's reading of him that we have here), rather than rejecting all concepts of human nature, just rejected those which he did not accept. This is certainly true, but weaker than the conceptual incompatibility first alleged. Soper refers to the danger of 'a false reduction of natural to social determinants' (p. 72) and speaks of human beings as 'biologically determined' and also 'naturally determined in various ways by virtue of a common biological structure' (p. 78); yet warns against 'a doctrine of innate dispositions characterizing "human nature"' (p. 96). She says that the social features always attached to biological characteristics 'in a real and important sense render the natural a cultural product'; but adds immediately that this 'does not mean that their explanation can be given wholly in terms of social relations' (p. 78). Such equivocation and confusion are everywhere and mar an otherwise valuable argument. Consumption is 'determined', if only indirectly, 'by anthropological factors', but seemingly not determined by an 'essential human nature' (p. 87). And having insisted, as I have indicated, that we *are* biologically determined, Soper later sets herself to answering the question: what is wrong with saying that we are? Her answer appears to be that what is wrong is that we may then be in danger of treating *social* determinants as natural ones – which amounts to holding that it is wrong to say that natural determinants are natural because it is wrong to say that social determinants are natural. Try generalizing this logic: one should not say that even numbers are divisible by two, because one might then say that odd numbers are, etc. Happily, Soper immediately goes on to say once again that we *are* biologically determined (pp. 95–96).

124. *Grundrisse*, p. 92.

Bibliography

1. *Writings of Marx and Engels*

Marx, K., *Capital*, Volume I, Harmondsworth 1976.
—*Capital*, Volume III, Moscow 1962.
—*A Contribution to the Critique of Political Economy*, London 1971.
—*Grundrisse*, Harmondsworth 1973.
—*Theories of Surplus Value*, 3 volumes, Moscow 1968–72.
—and Engels, F., *Collected Works*, Volumes 1–6, London 1975–76.
—and Engels, F., *Selected Works*, 3 volumes, Moscow 1969–70.

2. *Other Works Cited*

Althusser, L., *For Marx*, London 1969.
—and Balibar, E., *Reading Capital*, London 1970.
Beetham, D., 'Beyond Liberal Democracy', in Miliband, R., and Saville, J. (eds.), *The Socialist Register 1981*, London 1981.
Bottomore, T., 'Is There a Totalitarian View of Human Nature?', *Social Research*, Volume 40 No. 3, Autumn 1973.
—and Rubel, M. (eds.), *Karl Marx: Selected Writings in Sociology and Social Philosophy*, Harmondsworth 1963.
Callinicos, A., *Althusser's Marxism*, London 1976.
Cohen, G. A., *Karl Marx's Theory of History: A Defence*, Oxford 1978.
Collier, A., 'Materialism and Explanation in the Human Sciences', in Mepham, J., and Ruben, D. -H. (eds.), *Issues in Marxist Philosophy*, Volume 2, Brighton 1979.

—'Truth and Practice', *Radical Philosophy*, No. 5, Summer 1973.

Cumming, R. D., 'Is Man Still Man?', *Social Research*, Volume 40 No. 3, Autumn 1973.

Evans, M., *Karl Marx*, London 1975.

Fleischer, H., *Marxism and History*, London 1973.

Hook, S., *From Hegel to Marx*, Ann Arbor 1962.

Kamenka, E., *The Ethical Foundations of Marxism*, London 1972.

McLellan, D., *Karl Marx: His Life and Thought*, London 1973.

McMurtry, J., *The Structure of Marx's World-View*, Princeton 1978.

Mepham, J., 'Who Makes History?', *Radical Philosophy*, No. 6, Winter 1973.

Meszaros, I., *Marx's Theory of Alienation*, London 1970.

Moore, B., *Injustice. The Social Bases of Obedience and Revolt*, London 1978.

Ollman, B., *Alienation: Marx's Conception of Man in Capitalist Society*, Cambridge 1971.

Petrovic, G., *Marx in the Mid-Twentieth Century*, New York 1967.

Soper, K., 'Marxism, Materialism and Biology', in Mepham and Ruben (see Collier, A., above for details).

—'On Materialisms', *Radical Philosophy*, No. 15, Autumn 1976.

Suchting, W., 'Marx's *Theses on Feuerbach*: Notes Towards a Commentary', in Mepham and Ruben (see Collier, A., above for details).

Sumner, C., *Reading Ideologies*, London 1979.

Timpanaro, S., *On Materialism*, London 1975.

Tucker, R., *Philosophy and Myth in Karl Marx*, Cambridge 1961.

Venable, V., *Human Nature: The Marxian View*, Gloucester, Mass. 1975.

Index

Printed in the United States
by Baker & Taylor Publisher Services